the asian oven

the
asian oven

Innovative ways with Asian Food

Jo Marion Seow

Marshall Cavendish
Cuisine

Editor: Jolene Limuco
Designer: Lock Hong Liang
Photographer: Kiyoshi Yoshizawa, Jambu Studio

Published by Marshall Cavendish Cuisine
An imprint of Marshall Cavendish International

Other Marshall Cavendish Offices:
Marshall Cavendish International. PO Box 65829 London EC1P 1NY, UK • Marshall
Cavendish Corporation. 99 White Plains Road, Tarrytown NY 10591-9001, USA • Marshall
Cavendish International (Thailand) Co Ltd. 253 Asoke, 12th Flr, Sukhumvit 21 Road,
Klongtoey Nua, Wattana, Bangkok 10110, Thailand • Marshall Cavendish (Malaysia) Sdn
Bhd, Times Subang, Lot 46, Subang Hi-Tech Industrial Park, Batu Tiga, 40000 Shah Alam,
Selangor Darul Ehsan, Malaysia

Marshall Cavendish is a trademark of Times Publishing Limited

National Library Board Singapore Cataloguing in Publication Data

Seow, Jo Marion.
The Asian oven Innovative ways with Asian food / Jo Marion Seow. – Singapore :
Marshall Cavendish Cuisine, c2011.
p. cm.
ISBN : 978-981-4328-53-1

1. Electric cooking. 2. Cooking, Asian. I. Title.

TX827
641.586 — dc22   OCN697445068

Printed in Singapore by KWF Printing Pte Ltd

dedication

To Beth, Julia, Carrie,
Chris and Jordan

acknowledgements

Jolene: Thank you, thank you and thank you for your patience in making all the corrections; your assurance when I was so uncertain, and your help in washing all those dishes!

Hong Liang: Your ideas and creativity drive and inspire us all. You took a simple idea of cooking in the oven and really ran with it. This book is beautiful beyond what I imagined. It is indeed my privilege to work with you on this project.

Kiyoshi: Always cool, always calm; you were the anchor when we ran into a storm. Your artistic eye saw the photogenic potential in the most ordinary of food, making it extraordinary in your shots.

Guo Jie: Those times when we hit a wall, your ideas brought us through...thank you!

Bansoor and Rina: Thank you for sharing your recipes with me. Kin Lan, Evelyn, Chin, Swee Cher, Peggy, MJ, the two Irenes, May, Pat and Amy: Your care and heartfelt prayers for me are deeply appreciated.

Jon, Tim and Paul: Thank you for being the willing guinea pigs during the entire period of recipe testing.

Finally, I want to thank God for making all things possible.

CONTENTS

contents

introduction

People are invariably surprised when I tell them I cook my loh bak (braised pork in dark soy sauce) in the oven. Or that I fry my ha cheong kai (shrimp paste chicken wings) in the oven and not in a pot of oil.

Indeed, why cook Asian food in such a non-Asian kitchen appliance at all?

My fascination with ovens started long before I ever owned one, fuelled by those television mothers of the 1960s and 1970s bringing out their piece de resistance from the oven to deeply appreciative anticipation of their sitcom families. I aspired to be such a cook, outfitted in a clean crisp apron, bringing out a perfectly golden brown casserole to the oohs and ahs of my family.

When I finally purchased my own oven, I took flight—scaling heights never attempted before in my culinary journey. I was finally able to turn those lovely cookbook pictures of cakes, cookies and pies into real victuals I could sink my teeth into. The sugar junkie in me had never been more satisfied.

In Singapore, we tend to associate the use of the oven with baked goodies like cakes, pastries and bread. Of course we roast chickens and even turkeys in the oven too. As such, the usually dormant oven may be awakened to a flurry of activities during festive seasons.

After years of using the oven, my initial celluloid-inspired awe of it transformed into a practical appreciation of its versatility and the sheer variety of food that can be cooked in it.

The oven is such a multi-functional cooking appliance that it is a shame to use it only for the occasional baking and roasting. Or even worse, as an extension of storage space in the kitchen. In the West, many savoury dishes are cooked in the oven as a matter of course—baked fish, braised meats, roasted vegetables and even rice dishes. So why not cook Asian food in it?

This book is a result of my explorations and experimentations with the oven—a process that has accelerated my learning curve and produced some pretty delectable results. Many of the recipes here are familiar ones that are traditionally prepared over a stove fire, but can just as easily be done in the oven. I would go out on a limb and say that they are more easily cooked in the oven as once the food goes into the oven, I can stop fussing over it. The oven will do its job according to the temperature and timing I set.

There is something romantically alluring about food being quietly and gently cooked in the oven with its lovely aroma wafting through the home. As the food cooks, I can start washing up or get on with another dish.

No matter how many times I have used the oven, it is always with a sense of heightened anticipation when I open the oven door to bring the cooked dish out. It may be a pot of fragrant bubbling curry, a tray of beautifully browned crispy chicken wings or a heady aromatic pandan-coconut cake. Each of these is a Kodak moment spurring me to use the oven again.

I urge you to explore the diversity of Asian dishes that can be cooked in the multi-faceted oven. You will be pleasantly surprised.

getting to know your oven

Ovens are rather idiosyncratic appliances. Different brands of ovens differ slightly from one another in any number of ways—heat distribution and preheating, baking and roasting times. Even rack positions for particular types of baking and roasting are all variables you have to consider when comparing one oven to the next. In spite of these variables, the oven is surprisingly easy to use.

The first thing you should do is to keep the oven's instruction manual within reach in the kitchen. Everything you need to know about your particular oven is in there. Read through it thoroughly and refer to it whenever you are unsure of anything.

You need to add your practical working knowledge of your oven to the technical information found in the manual. Evidently the only way you can acquire that is to use it. Banish all fear of making mistakes right from the start. Making mistakes is probably the best way to learn something. I remember my errors more clearly than my successes as I have no desire to commit the same blunders twice.

Start with a simple dish, perhaps a familiar one you have cooked before on the stove. See how it turns out in the oven. Write comments about the outcome of the dish, both the positive and the negative. Perhaps your fried chicken wings took a few minutes less than the recommended cooking time to be perfectly cooked and nicely browned. Make a note of that. This could possibly mean that the heat distribution in your oven is more efficient than mine. How about the marinade—a little too salty for your taste? Not spicy enough? Or is it just right? Jot that down too. The next time you cook this dish again, your notes will serve as a useful guide.

Another thing to take note of is whether your oven is fan-assisted. Cookbooks normally give temperatures for conventional ovens without fan assistance. The fan distributes heat faster and more evenly. Hence for such ovens, the given temperatures must be adjusted 15°C (59°F) to 20°C (68°F) lower.

Whether you are a newbie or an old hand at using the oven, the crucial point is that practise really does make perfect.

oven cookware and cooking aids

All the dishes in this book were prepared using the cookware I have acquired over the years. Granted, I have amassed quite a lot—a fair number of which I received as gifts. But I find myself employing the same few pieces over and over. So you do not really need to purchase the entire range of cookware in order to use the oven.

To start off, maximise your oven's potential by having one set of the biggest cookware that can fit into it—from pots to roasting tins.

For cooking stews, pots made of stainless steel, enamel, stone, porcelain, clay, glass or cast iron can all be used. They should preferably come with tight-fitting lids. Plastic knobs or handles may run the risk of melting in the hot oven. I wrap any plastic parts with aluminium foil and they have not suffered any ill effects as stews are usually cooked at moderately low temperatures of between 150°C (300°F) and 160°C (325°F). You need just one big pot that can take the food from stove to oven. In all probability, you already own one.

My built-in oven can hold two smaller pots or casserole dishes at the same time. This means two different dishes can be cooked simultaneously. I often have a pot of curry and a pot of green bean soup sharing oven space as these two dishes cook at the same temperature for a similar length of time. If your oven can't accommodate two pieces of cookware, it is still a good idea to acquire at least one smaller pot for cooking a lesser quantity of food. That small pot you use to cook instant noodles? That will do nicely.

Five-cup and 10-cup capacity casserole dishes are used in some of the recipes in this book. Casserole dishes are wonderful to have whether or not you use them as oven cookware. They are usually microwave- and oven-safe, not too costly and excellent to serve food in. Invest in a couple of these.

For baking cookies, you need at least two trays—one tray of cookies can go in the oven while you work on the next. Trays are multi-functional—they are good for roasting meats, root vegetables, baking bread, holding cups of crème brûlée and can even be used as serving platters. I wrap my very used tray with aluminium foil and serve rows of colourful salad vegetables in it.

As for cake tins, I have been using my 22-cm (8¹/₂-in) square tin for umpteenth years now. I prefer baking a big cake as opposed to a small one as both require the same amount of effort. The extra cake will be tightly wrapped and frozen. I have a thing for ergonomically shaped food parcels that can fit into the freezer nicely, hence the square cake tin. If you prefer round cakes, a 23-cm (9-in) round tin is a good substitute for the 22-cm (8¹/₂-in) square.

For sizable pies and cheesecakes, a 22-cm (8¹/₂-in) springform tin works very well. The sides of the tin are easily removed to unveil these gorgeous bakes.

One 12-cup muffin tray will suffice unless you are really into baking muffins.

A 23 x 13 x 8-cm (9 x 5 x 3-in) loaf tin is good for baking bread and cakes. I have even used this loaf tin for lasagne as it is deep enough to contain four to five layers of lasagne.

For roasting, my deep roasting tin measuring 37 x 26 x 5-cm (14 x 10 x 2-in) can hold two chickens, each weighing about 1.2 kg (2 lb 6 oz). When cooking for a large group, this big tin can also be used for recipes like Dum Chicken Briyani and other baked rice or pasta dishes. However this tin will not fit into a countertop oven. For that, a 28 x 20 x 5-cm (11 x 7 x 2-in) tin is a good option. Your roasting tins may have slightly different dimensions from mine, give or take a centimetre or two. These minor deviations will not affect the cooking adversely.

A 23-cm (9-in) round, glass flan dish is used for the egg custard recipes. Otah and quiches can also be baked and served in it.

It is good to have at least a couple of racks. Breads, cakes, cookies and pizzas must be cooled on racks to allow for air circulation, without which the bottoms of these bakes will turn soggy.

Besides cookware, aluminium foil and non-stick baking paper are absolute essentials. The former is used to line trays and roasting tins, making washing up a breeze. The latter is an indispensable godsend and works like a charm. Nothing sticks to it. It can be used to line almost every tray and tin that goes into the oven. Cake tins lined with it will not require any greasing with softened butter. The non-stick paper is easily peeled off the cake later.

Finally, to retrieve the hot dishes from the oven, a pair of mittens is required. A dry towel, folded several times lengthwise, is just as effective in insulating the heat from delicate hands.

cleaning the oven

Instructions on cleaning can be found in the manufacturer's manual. It is not necessary to clean the oven after every use, especially after cooking or baking food that does not splatter like stews or cakes. However when the oven is used to fry and roast, it should be cleaned when it has cooled. Follow the manual's suggestions on cleaning agents and scrubs suitable for your particular oven. It is not a good idea to allow splattered grease to accumulate as the layers of grease will congeal, making it difficult to clean. The most crucial thing to remember is that the electricity must be turned off before any cleaning can commence.

cooking basics

Pandan juice, *gula melaka* syrup, sambal *belacan* and fried shallots are ingredients used in a number of recipes in this book. These basic ingredients require a little time to prepare, but store very well in the fridge or freezer. It is worth the time and effort to make a big batch of these, and keep them in the fridge or freezer for future use.

Pandan Juice
Wash 2 to 3 bunches of pandan leaves (about 100 g / 3½ oz). Cut the leaves into short segments and transfer all to a blender. Add 250 ml (8 fl oz / 1 cup) of water and blend the leaves to a fine pulp. Strain the juice through a fine sieve into a container. Squeeze out as much juice as possible from the pulp before discarding it.

Store the juice in 4 Tbsp portions in clean plastic bags. Alternatively store in small plastic containers with the lids on and freeze.

Gula Melaka Syrup
When buying *gula melaka*, check the ingredient list, which should consist of only one item: palm sugar. Any other additions or worse, the absence of palm sugar would mean an adulterated product that tastes nothing like the real deal. Real *gula melaka* has a slight coconut fragrance whereas the fake stuff simply tastes like brown sugar.

To make the syrup, finely grate or chop 100g (3½ oz) *gula melaka*. Add 4 Tbsp water and heat over a small flame till the *gula melaka* dissolves. Turn off the flame immediately. If the syrup is allowed to continue boiling, it will develop a burnt taste.

Bottled Sambal *Belacan*
This is a fried chilli paste that consists of chillies, shallots, garlic, lemongrass, galangal, turmeric and *belacan* (fermented prawns). There is an inordinate amount of chilli oil (about one-third of the contents) that should be removed. The oil only adds colour and spiciness to a dish without the flavours that the other ingredients bring. Degreasing the chilli paste first will result in a more concentrated paste, packing in all the flavours.

Place a stack of 4 to 5 pieces of kitchen towels on a plate. Skim off as much oil as possible from the chilli paste. Spread the paste on the kitchen towels and leave for 15–20 minutes. The oil will be absorbed by the kitchen towels. Spoon the chilli paste back into the bottle. It is now ready for use.

Fried Shallots
Fried shallots are the indispensable garnish of choice for a variety of our local dishes. The oil that the shallots are fried in can be drizzled over porridge or soup, infusing the dish with its inimitable fragrance. Ready-fried shallots are easily available but I have never liked the taste of these commercially produced shallots—they lack the fragrance of home-fried shallots, and worse, sometimes they even taste rancid!

To make fried shallots, thinly slice about 20 peeled shallots. Heat 250 ml (8 fl oz / 1 cup) oil in a small saucepan or pot. Add all the shallot slices at once. Add more oil if necessary to completely cover the shallots. Fry over medium heat, stirring often. When the shallots turn light golden, turn off the flame immediately. The shallots will continue to fry in the residual heat of the hot oil to a gloriously golden brown hue.

Use a metal strainer or slotted spoon to remove the shallots from the oil, draining off as much of the oil as possible. Place the shallots on kitchen towels to cool completely before storing in a jar. Keep the fragrant shallot oil in a separate jar. Store both jars in the fridge to keep the contents from turning rancid.

steam

In the oven, heat is transferred to the food through radiation, air convection and conduction. This dry heat method of cooking gives baked food and roasts that tantalisingly brown exterior. Steaming, on the other hand, is a moist heat method in which food is cooked by the steam generated from rapidly boiling water. How then do we steam in the oven?

As long as there is sufficient fluid in the food (in the form of water or stock) and/or the food is well covered to prevent the escape of steam, then steaming is possible. As the food cooks, it will generate its own steam which keeps the food moist.

Seafood benefits from this temperate cooking method. Fish, shellfish and crustaceans can all be steamed in the oven. When cooking whole crabs in the oven, the shells provide their own covering, holding in a lot of juices. Other delicate food like eggs and egg custards adapt just as well to the oven as they have high water content. To ensure even cooking, the food must be at room temperature when it goes into the oven.

Steaming in the oven actually negates the need to top up water during the cooking process. Need I mention how much easier it is to remove the steamed dish from the oven, than from a steamer? The food is served in the dish it is steamed in. There is no steamer to be washed, nor is there a need to clean the oven as steaming is splatter-free.

simple selar with spicy dip *serves 2*

Any fish that is conventionally cooked in a steamer can be "steamed" in the oven. Preheating is not even necessary for this dish. The fish is placed in a baking dish or plate and tightly covered with aluminium foil to prevent the skin from drying out. The whole dish is then put into the oven to cook. It is as simple as that.

Horse mackerel (selar)	2, about 200 g (7 oz) each
Bird's eye chilli	1, seeded and minced
Garlic	1 clove, peeled and minced
Shallot	1, peeled and finely diced
Kalamansi limes	2, juice only
Fermented prawn (shrimp) paste (*cincalok*)	1 Tbsp

- Line a baking dish with non-stick baking paper.

- Make a couple of diagonal cuts on each side of the fish. Place both fish in the baking dish. Cover the dish tightly with foil.

- Switch on the oven to 200°C (400°F). Put the fish into the oven and cook for 20 minutes.

- Mix the chilli, garlic and shallot with the lime juice and fermented prawn paste.

- Serve the cooked fish immediately with the spicy dip.

stingray with tom yum paste *serves 4*

You need to get the stingray in big pieces, and then have the fishmonger cut each into half horizontally. Any other boneless fish fillet can be a good substitute. A whole fish though is a bother to eat in a recipe like this in which the fish is smothered with a paste. Plenty of hiding places in the paste for nasty little bones.

Stingray fillets	2, about 250 g (9 oz) each, cut in half horizontally
Tom yum paste	2 Tbsp
Water	2 Tbsp
Sugar	1 tsp
Banana leaves or aluminium foil	8 pieces
Kaffir lime leaves	2
Shallots	4, peeled and thinly sliced
Red chilli	1, seeded and thinly sliced

- Preheat the oven to 200°C (400°F).

- You will need 2 pieces of banana leaves or foil for each piece of fish. Blanch the leaves in boiling water first to make them malleable.

- Mix the *tom yum* paste with water and sugar.

- Put 2 pieces of banana leaves or foil together, one on top of the other. Place 1 piece of stingray on the banana leaf or foil. Spread a quarter of the *tom yum* mixture on the fish. Fold the banana leaves or foil over the fish to form a parcel. If using banana leaves, secure the ends of the parcel with toothpicks. Repeat with the remaining ingredients.

- Place the parcels on a tray and bake for 15 minutes. Although I use the word "bake" here, the fish fillets are essentially being steamed as a lot of moisture is retained inside the parcels.

- In the meantime, prepare the kaffir lime leaves by cutting off the central stalks, and then slice the leaves thinly.

- When the stingray is cooked, open the parcels. Sprinkle the lime leaves, shallots and chilli over the fish. Serve hot.

halibut with salted soy bean paste *serves 4*

Salted soy beans (*tau cheo*) is a seasoning often used for cooking fish. My grandfather often ate steamed fish with salted soy beans, instead of soy sauce as a dip. In this recipe, the salted soy beans are mashed with grated ginger and garlic to make an even more flavourful seasoning.

The halibut comes ready skinned and de-boned, making this an easy recipe to prepare. Again, any other fish fillet can be used in place of halibut. There is no need to wrap the fish in aluminium foil as the moist salted soy bean paste will ensure that the fish does not dry out.

Halibut fillets	4, about 150 g (5 oz) each
Salted soy beans (*tau cheo*)	3 Tbsp
Garlic	1 clove, peeled and grated
Ginger	1 thumb-size knob, peeled and grated
Sugar	2 tsp
Cooking oil	2 tsp
Spring onion (scallion)	1, sliced

- Preheat the oven to 200°C (400°F). Line a baking dish with non-stick baking paper.

- Place halibut fillets in the baking dish in a single layer.

- Mash salted soy beans with the back of a spoon. Mix garlic, ginger, mashed salted soy beans, sugar and oil. Spread this mixture in an even layer on the halibut fillets. Bake in the oven for 6–8 minutes.

- To check if the fish is cooked, insert a fork into the thickest part of the fillet. If the fish breaks up easily, it is done. Otherwise, bake for a further 1–2 minutes.

- Once the fish is cooked, sprinkle spring onion on top and serve immediately.

snapper with ginger-garlic sauce *serves 4*

An essential component of many recipes across cuisines, the garlic is a fascinating ingredient to cook with. It can be mind-blowingly pungent and spicy when raw but mellow with a nuanced creaminess when gently cooked. In this ginger-garlic sauce, the garlic is only mildly cooked by the heat from the hot oil, retaining some of its nipping tang. This sauce goes over well with any kind of steamed fish, whole or filleted. It can also be added to stir-fried fish or chicken slices.

Ginger	1 thumb-size knob
Garlic	2 large cloves, peeled
Spring onion (scallion)	1, diced
Cooking oil	$1^1/_2$ Tbsp
Light soy sauce	2 Tbsp
Snapper fillets	4, about 150 g (5 oz) each

- Scrape the skin off the ginger using a spoon. The rounded edge of the spoon is able to navigate the curved surfaces of the ginger and remove just the skin.

- Finely grate the ginger and the garlic. Put the grated ingredients and spring onion into a small bowl.

- Heat oil in a small saucepan until it is smoking hot. Pour the oil onto the ingredients in the bowl and give everything a stir. Now add light soy sauce and stir to combine. The sauce is done.

- Preheat the oven to 200°C (400°F).

- Place fish in a casserole dish. Cover tightly with foil and bake for 6–8 minutes.

- Remove the cooked fish from the oven. Discard the foil.

- Spoon the ginger-garlic sauce over the fish and serve immediately.

squid with lime juice *serves 4*

For this clean, uncluttered dish of steamed squid with nothing more than kalamansi lime juice, fish sauce and chillies, only squid of optimum freshness can be considered. There is just no place for mediocrity to hide in simple steamed dishes like this. And better yet if the squid is also thick and juicy.

Squid	1, about 350 g (12 oz)
Kalamansi limes	6, squeezed to obtain 2 Tbsp juice
Red chilli	1, seeded and chopped
Garlic	1 clove, peeled and chopped
Fish sauce	2 tsp
Sugar	1 tsp

- Preheat the oven to 220°C (425°F).

- Carefully pull out the head of the squid. The ink bag and guts will follow. Cut off the eyes and ink bag. Squeeze out the beak and discard. Pull out the gill and peel off the skin from the squid tube.

- Wash the tentacles and squid tube well. Put these in a casserole dish. Cook in the oven for 8–9 minutes. Remove from the oven immediately.

- Mix lime juice, chilli and garlic together with fish sauce and sugar.

- Once the squid has cooled enough to handle, use a fork to remove it from the dish to a cutting board. Slice the squid and tentacles. Return the cut pieces to the dish. Pour the sauce over the squid and serve immediately.

prawns with garlic *serves 4*

Just like the squid in the previous recipe, only the most sparklingly fresh prawns can make this dish sing. Because the prawns are ready so quickly, that means the garlic is only mildly cooked, and hence retains quite a bit of its sharp piquant bite. Garlic lovers would want all six or maybe more cloves of garlic in this recipe.

Large prawns (shrimps)	12, about 450 g (1 lb)
Garlic	4–6 cloves, peeled and grated
Spring onion (scallion)	1, cut into thin strips
Light soy sauce	to taste

- Snip off the feelers and the pointy shell above the prawn heads. Wash and drain the prawns well.

- Use a pair of kitchen scissors to make a slit down each prawn's back. Remove the vein.

- Preheat the oven to 180°C (350°F).

- Stuff the garlic into the slits of the prawns. Arrange the prawns in a single layer in a baking dish.

- Cook in the oven for 10–12 minutes. Remove them immediately from the oven once they are cooked.

- Sprinkle spring onion over the prawns. Serve with light soy sauce on the side.

steamed triple egg *serves 4–5*

What an ingenious idea, this! Who could have predicted the fabulously delectable outcome of combining three different kinds of eggs? The regular hen's egg, duck's egg and century egg come together to form a beautiful palette of yellow, mottled with deep oranges and dark browns in this dish.

You don't have to buy an entire tray of duck eggs or century eggs if these aren't regular ingredients in your cooking. Instead purchase a single salted duck's egg and a single century egg from the dried goods stall at the wet market.

All the ingredients, except for the cup of water, should be at room temperature. This will shorten cooking time in the oven, and allow the eggs to set more evenly.

A 23-cm (9-in) glass flan or pie dish is the most appropriate and pretty dish to cook and serve this in. The egg mixture will fill this dish to a depth of almost 2-cm (1-in) and cook in about 25 minutes. Any dish smaller than this means the heat has to penetrate a deeper layer of the egg mixture, resulting in not just a longer cooking time, but also overcooking the sides while the centre of the eggs may still be runny. If you don't have a glass dish, you can cook this in a metal cake tin of similar dimensions. Or like my mama, use an enamel dish.

Minced pork	100 g (3$^1/_2$ oz)
Water	2 Tbsp
Light soy sauce	2 tsp
Ground white pepper	$^1/_4$ tsp
Salted duck egg	1
Century egg	1, shelled
Eggs	2
Very hot water	250 ml (8 fl oz / 1 cup)
Salt	$^1/_4$ tsp
Ground white pepper	a dash

- Mix the minced pork together with water, light soy sauce and pepper.

- Preheat the oven to 180°C (350°F). Have a 23-cm (9-in) glass flan or pie dish, or cake tin at hand.

- Break the duck egg into a mixing bowl. Take the yolk out, dice it and return to the bowl.

- Dice the century egg and put this into the mixing bowl as well. Crack the eggs directly into the bowl. Add the seasoned minced pork. Mix everything well with a fork, breaking up the minced pork as you go.

- Now add the salt and a quarter of the hot water while stirring constantly to prevent the eggs from being scrambled. Finally pour the rest of the water into the eggs as you continue to stir and distribute the hot water evenly into the mixture. Pour into the dish or tin.

- Bake in the oven for 25–30 minutes. Remove from the oven once the egg mixture is cooked. Serve.

egg tofu with minced pork *serves 4–6*

This is homemade egg tofu that is "steamed" in the oven. It is soft and velvety, quite different from the agar-agar-like texture of the commercially manufactured variety. The minced pork is fried separately then placed on the steamed tofu. For a spicy version, include a teaspoonful or more of drained sambal *belacan* to the minced pork. The non-spicy version is good with porridge while the spicy one with rice.

Eggs	4
Unsweetened soy bean milk	250 ml (8 fl oz / 1 cup)
Canned chicken broth	4 Tbsp
Salt	$^1/_2$ tsp

Topping

Minced pork	100 g (3$^1/_2$ oz)
Water	3 Tbsp
Light soy sauce	1 tsp
Sugar	1 tsp
Dried shiitake mushrooms	2 large, rinsed and soaked
Salted soy beans (*tau cheo*)	$^1/_2$ Tbsp, including a bit of the liquid
Cooking oil	1 Tbsp
Garlic	1 clove, peeled and minced
Botted sambal *belacan* (optional)	1–2 tsp
Corn flour (cornstarch)	1 tsp, mixed with 2 Tbsp water
Spring onion (scallion)	1, diced

- Preheat the oven to 180°C (350°F). Get ready a 23-cm (9-in) flan dish.

- Break the eggs into a mixing bowl.

- Heat the soy bean milk, chicken broth and salt over the stove or in the microwave oven until just before boiling point. Pour about a quarter of the liquid into the eggs, vigorously stirring (not beating as we don't want to incorporate too much air) to avoid scrambling the eggs. Now pour another quarter of the liquid into the eggs, again stirring well. Finally mix in the rest of the liquid. Pour this into the flan dish and "steam" uncovered in the oven for 25 minutes.

- In the meantime, prepare the minced pork topping. Combine the minced pork with water, light soy sauce and sugar.

- Drain the mushrooms but do not squeeze out any water from the mushrooms. Dice the mushrooms.

- Mash the salted soy beans with the flat bottom of a Chinese soup spoon. This amount is too small to warrant trotting out the blender.

- Heat the oil in a wok and fry the mushrooms. We want the mushrooms to take on a deep brown patina. When the mushrooms are caramelised this way, their flavour is deepened.

- Remove the mushrooms from the oil. Add the salted soy beans to the remaining oil (adding more oil if needed) and fry for a few seconds. Add the minced garlic and sambal *belacan* (if using). Fry for a few more seconds until fragrant. Now include minced pork and mushrooms, stirring well and breaking up the clumps of pork. Finally add the corn flour mixture and cook a few more seconds.

- When the tofu is done, remove it from the oven. Top with the minced pork and sprinkle on the spring onion.

japanese steamed egg chawanmushi *serves 4*

This Japanese steamed egg is cooked in individual teacups, just like the ones in the restaurants, complete with the slices of shiitake mushroom, which float on the surface of the liquid custard. The dry heat of the oven will dehydrate and brown the mushroom just a little, resulting in a more intense flavour.

Bonito flakes	2 Tbsp
Water or chicken stock	250 ml (8 fl oz / 1 cup)
Salt	1/4 tsp
Eggs	3, at room temperature
Fresh shiitake mushrooms	2, stalks removed and sliced into 4 pieces
Spring onion (scallion)	1, diced

- To make bonito stock or dashi, combine bonito flakes and water or chicken stock in a pot and bring it to a boil. Turn off the flame. Let the flavours infuse till the flakes sink to the bottom.

- Preheat the oven to 180°C (350°F). Place 4 Chinese teacups on a baking tray.

- Strain the soup stock into a mixing bowl. Press out all the flavourful broth from the bonito flakes. Discard the flakes.

- Add 1/4 tsp salt if you used water to make the dashi, less if chicken stock was used. Break the eggs into the stock. Stir gently to mix. We want to avoid making too many bubbles. Taste and add more salt if necessary.

- Divide the egg mixture among the teacups. Top with mushrooms and spring onion. Cook in the oven for 12–15 minutes. The centre of the custard should be slightly wobbly when cooked. Serve immediately.

salted chicken yeem kai *serves 6–8*

Recipes for salted chicken usually call for several kilograms of salt in which the chicken is encrusted. Some recipes require the salt to be fried first, all of which mean too much salt and labour!

But what about brining? Isn't the objective to get the salinity right into the chicken meat? Brining would definitely accomplish that. If I wrap the brined chicken tightly in foil and cook it in the oven, it will effectively be steamed inside that concealed parcel. No need for a steamer or a pot of boiling water.

For the brining, you need a container that allows the chicken to be completely immersed in the brine. To find out the amount of brine required, place the chicken in the container. Add the water, cup by cup till the chicken is immersed with about a centimetre of water above. You'll need to hold the chicken down, as it is a little buoyant. Once you have measured the water, calculate the amount of salt needed in the proportion of $1^1/_2$ Tbsp salt for each cup of water.

I use a deep mixing bowl and need only 1 litre (32 fl oz / 4 cups) of water for the chicken to be completely submerged. A heavy object like a plate will help to keep the chicken down.

Chicken	1, about 1.2 kg (2 lb 6 oz) with skin on
Water	as needed
Salt	as needed
White peppercorns	2 Tbsp
Spring onion (scallion)	1, cut into long thin strips

- Wash the chicken well and set aside in the container it will be brined in. Pour in water, 1 cup at a time till the chicken is completely immersed. Note down the amount of water and calculate the quantity of salt needed in the ratio of $1^1/_2$ Tbsp salt for every cup of water.

- Discard the water, leaving the chicken in the container. Keep the chicken in the fridge while you prepare the brine.

- Put the peppercorns in a pot. Using a pestle, gently crush the white peppercorns to release the flavour. There is no need to pound the peppercorns. Add 500 ml (16 fl oz / 2 cups) water and turn on the heat. When the water boils, cover the pot and simmer gently for 10 minutes. Turn off the flame.

- Reserve 2 Tbsp of the peppery liquid. Strain the peppery liquid and measure the amount. Top up with cold water to make up the total amount needed to brine the chicken. Add the required amount of salt. Stir until all the salt is dissolved. Let the brine cool completely. You can speed up the process by putting the brine in the fridge.

- Once the brine has cooled, lower the chicken into it. Balance a heavy object on the chicken to keep it submerged. Cover with cling film and leave in the fridge to brine for 3 hours. Over brining will result in a very salty chicken.

- When the brining is complete, discard the brine. Rinse the chicken under running water to rid it of excess brine on its surface. The chicken needs to lose the chill and be at room temperature when it goes into the oven. This will take 3–5 hours depending on the room temperature. If you are not planning to cook it in the next few hours, return it to the fridge and take it out 3–5 hours before cooking.

- Preheat the oven to 240°C (475°F) or 220°C (425°F) for a fan-assisted oven.

- Place a piece of non-stick baking paper on a large sheet of aluminium foil. Put the chicken on the paper, and pour the 2 Tbsp of reserved peppery liquid over the chicken. Fold the foil to encase the chicken. All edges should be tightly sealed. Place this whole parcel on a tray and cook in the oven for 40 minutes.

- Once the chicken is cooked, remove the tray from the oven. Let the chicken rest for 20–30 minutes without opening the parcel.

- Get a small bowl and a serving plate ready. Open the parcel and transfer the chicken to the serving plate. Pour the meat juices from the foil into a small bowl.

- Cut the chicken up with a pair of kitchen scissors. Skim off the oil from the meat juices and pour this peppery juice over the chicken. Garnish with spring onion. Serve.

green curry otah *serves 8*

Green curry *otah* is an interesting way to eat green curry. The flavours are the same, but the textures are wholly different—something reminiscent of smooth custard. The colours have to be the best part of this dish. A refreshing change from the familiar orange *otah*, this one is orange-red (the cooked prawns) on a bed of gentle green.

For ease of preparation and eating, the prawns can be shelled, de-veined, and then placed flat on the *otah*. To achieve a prettier dish (as in the picture), all it takes is a little cosmetic surgery on the prawns.

Mackerel fillet	1, 200 g (7 oz), sliced	Dried prawn (shrimp) paste (*belacan*)	1 tsp
Medium prawns (shrimps)	16	Water	4 Tbsp
Galangal	1 thumb-size knob, peeled and thinly sliced	Coconut powder	50 g (2 oz)
Lemongrass	1 stalk, about 5-cm (2-in) from the root end, thinly sliced	Coriander powder	1 tsp
		Ground white pepper	1 tsp
Coriander leaves (cilantro)	1 stalk, chopped	Cumin powder	$1/2$ tsp
Kaffir lime leaves	8	Fish sauce	4 tsp
Green bird's eye chilli	4, seeded	Sugar	1 Tbsp
		Eggs	5
Shallots	4, peeled	Banana leaves (optional)	2 pieces, 24 x 24-cm (9$1/2$ x 9$1/2$-in) each, for lining tray
Garlic	2 cloves, peeled		

- Prepare fish and leave to chill in the fridge.

- Shell the prawns, but retain the tail shell. Cut a slit down the length of each prawn and remove the vein. Pierce the tip of a paring knife in the middle of this slit and make a small cut. Push the tail shell of the prawn through this cut. Chill the prawns well in the fridge. This will help to prevent overcooking later on.

- Put galangal, lemongrass and coriander in a blender.

- Remove the central vein from each of the kaffir lime leaves. Throw half of these leaves into the blender and thinly slice the rest. Set the sliced leaves aside for later.

- To the ingredients in the blender, add the rest of the ingredients and 1 egg. Blend until a smooth paste is obtained. Pour this into a mixing bowl.

- Stir in the sliced kaffir lime leaves and the remaining eggs with a spatula.

- Preheat the oven to 180°C (350°F).

- Line the bottom and sides of a 22-cm (8$1/2$-in) square cake tin with double layers of banana leaves, if using. Make some cuts at the corners of each leaf so they fit snugly into the tin; or line with aluminium foil followed by non-stick baking paper.

- Pour blended mixture into the tin. Arrange fish slices in the tin. Position the prawns on top of the fish in 4 rows with 4 prawns in each row. The tails should all be pointing in the same direction. You may need to shift the fish slices so each prawn can sit on the fish.

- "Steam" the *otah* for 30 minutes. To serve, cut into 16 squares.

nyonya dumpling casserole *serves 8–10*

Making rice dumplings, whether it is *kiam bakh zhang* (savoury rice dumpling) or Nyonya dumpling, is an arduous process that requires a few days of relentless work. There are several parts to the whole process—from washing the bamboo leaves to preparing each ingredient for the filling. The dumplings also require several hours of cooking in boiling water.

Of course I never got round to making dumplings until it dawned on me to simplify the age-old method of preparation. I could simply make it in a tray by layering the rice and the filling. The casserole will essentially be steamed in the oven, as it will be tightly wrapped in foil, thereby sealing in all the steam.

When preparing a recipe that requires a certain amount of effort, it is often expedient to break up and space out the preparation. You would be amazed at how less demanding the whole process becomes.

Since discovering this much easier method, I have made Nyonya dumpling several times in the last couple of years. Bring a tray of this Nyonya dumpling to your next pot luck and hear the gasps of surprise when you unveil your creation.

Filling

Shallots	500 g (1 lb 1 1/2 oz)
Lean pork	500 g (1 lb 1 1/2 oz)
Water	as needed
Coriander seeds	50 g (2 oz)
Cooking oil	4 Tbsp
Garlic	8 cloves, peeled and minced
Dark soy sauce	1/2 Tbsp
Salt	1 1/4 tsp
Sugar	90 g (3 oz)

Rice

Glutinous rice	500 g (1 lb 1 1/2 oz)
Pandan juice (page 13)	125 ml (4 fl oz / 1/2 cup)
Cooking oil	2 Tbsp
Salt	1 tsp
Ground white pepper	1/2 tsp
Dried bamboo leaves	15–16 pieces, washed and soaked until soft

- Start some of the preparations a day ahead. Peel and wash the shallots. Slice the shallots thinly—about the thickness of a dollar coin. Keep them in a bag, seal tightly and store in the fridge.

- Put the pork in a small pot. Add 500 ml (16 fl oz / 2 cups) water and bring to a boil. Lower the heat and simmer gently with the pot covered for 30 minutes. Leave the pork to cool in the broth.

- When the pork has cooled sufficiently to be handled, take it out from the broth. Dice the pork into 1-cm ($^1/_2$-in) cubes. Keep the diced pork in a sealed bag or airtight container and leave in the fridge. Refrigerate the pork broth as well.

- The next day, wash the rice and leave to soak for at least 1 hour. Drain before using.

- Dry-fry the coriander seeds in a saucepan over a small flame. Give the saucepan a shake every now and then to toss the coriander seeds around. When you hear popping sounds from the coriander seeds, they are ready. Turn off the flame. Let the seeds cool. Grind the seeds finely in a blender once they are cooled.

- Measure the pork broth and top up with water to make 625 ml (20 fl oz / 2$^1/_2$ cups). Add pandan juice to this to get a total of 750 ml (24 fl oz / 3 cups) liquid.

- In a non-stick wok or frying pan, heat 4 Tbsp oil over a small to medium flame and fry the shallots. If the flame is too hot, parts of the shallots will burn before they can caramelise properly. Fry, stirring frequently until the shallots are evenly browned. Add the minced garlic and fry until it starts to brown. Now include the ground coriander seeds. Stir to mix everything well and fry for about 30 seconds before turning off the flame. Remove one-quarter of these aromatic ingredients and set aside to be used for the glutinous rice later.

- Turn on the flame again. To the remaining fried ingredients in the wok, add the diced pork. Stir to mix well. Add the dark soy sauce, 500 ml (16 fl oz / 2 cups) water, salt and sugar. Mix well and let the pork simmer uncovered for about 30 minutes or longer until it is tender. Most of the liquid should be evaporated when the pork is softened. The filling should be moist and tender. Transfer the filling to a large bowl.

- Line the bottom and sides of a 30 x 20 x 5-cm (11 x 7 x 2-in) baking tin with some bamboo leaves, overlapping them to cover the tin properly. Cut and trim the leaves so they fit the tin nicely.

- To cook the rice, heat 2 Tbsp oil in the wok. Return the fried shallots, garlic and ground coriander seeds that were set aside earlier to the wok. Add the drained rice. Mix the rice well with the oil and aromatics.

- Lower the heat and add 625 ml (20 fl oz / 2$^1/_2$ cups) broth and pandan juice mixture. Stir the rice and broth every now and then. Let the rice absorb the broth slowly. It is crucial that the flame is kept low or the liquid will evaporate too quickly and the rice would not absorb sufficient liquid.

- Preheat the oven to 180°C (350°F).

- Once the liquid is almost absorbed, transfer half of the partially cooked rice to the prepared tray. To the remaining rice in the wok, add the remaining broth and pandan juice mixture. Stir and let this rice absorb the extra liquid slowly over a low flame. Since this rice will form the top layer, it will need to absorb a bit more moisture to ensure that it will cook properly later on.

- In the meantime, use a spatula to level the rice in the tray. Top the first layer of rice with the filling. Again, level the filling with the spatula.

- While you are layering the casserole, keep an eye on the rice in the wok. When the liquid is almost absorbed, turn off the flame. Transfer this rice to the tray. Spread the rice out to cover the filling. Level the top. Cover the rice with the remaining bamboo leaves.

- Finally cover the tray with a large piece of aluminium foil, sealing all the edges tightly to prevent any steam from escaping as the casserole cooks.

- Cook the casserole in the preheated oven for 45 minutes. Let it sit covered in the oven for another 15 minutes with the heat turned off before serving.

dum chicken briyani *serves 6*

Dum chicken briyani hails from the Indian city of Hyderabad. In this dish, the chicken or mutton is marinated and cooked together with the rice. Even though no curry is served with it, it is every bit as flavourful as our local nasi briyani.

All the dum briyani recipes I have come across call for the rice to be half-cooked in plenty of water before being layered with the meat and cooked together. But the instructions on cooking the rice tend to be arbitrary. They hinge on several unspecified variables like intensity of heat and length of cooking time, both of which affect how much water the rice absorbs. There are also the determinants for half-cooked rice. What is half-cooked rice like as opposed to a third or two-thirds-cooked?

In tweaking this recipe, my primary concern was to determine ways to manage the aforementioned variables so that the window for error can be significantly reduced. I decided that the easiest way to accomplish this was to control the amount of water the rice absorbed.

Instead of partially cooking the rice in plenty of boiling water, I soak the rice for an hour first. The rice is then simmered in 500 ml (16 fl oz / 2 cups) of the liquid with the lid on. This minimises any moisture loss due to evaporation, and gives the rice time to gradually absorb the liquid.

When the rice is cooked with the chicken in a tightly sealed dish in the oven, it will continue to absorb moisture released by the meat juices and the marinade.

Basmati rice	525 g (18$\frac{1}{2}$ oz)
Chicken legs	4, about 200 g (7 oz) each, cut into 4 pieces
Milk	250 ml (8 fl oz / 1 cup)
Water	250 ml (8 fl oz / 1 cup)
Salt	1 tsp
Butter	30 g (1 oz)
Ginger	4 slices
Cinnamon sticks	2
Cardamom pods	4
Cloves	4
Orange food colouring	a few drops

Garnish

Fried shallots	25 g (1 oz)
Roasted cashew nuts	100 g (3$\frac{1}{2}$ oz)
Coriander leaves (cilantro)	1 stalk, roughly chopped

Seasoning

Ginger	1 large thumb-size knob, peeled and grated
Garlic	4 cloves, peeled and grated
Coriander leaves (cilantro)	1 large stalk, roughly chopped
Salt	1 tsp
Chilli powder	2 tsp
Coriander powder	2 tsp
Cumin powder	1 tsp
Turmeric powder	1 tsp
Ground white pepper	1 tsp
Fried shallots	25 g (1 oz)
Yoghurt	250 ml (8 fl oz / 1 cup)
Cinnamon stick	1
Cardamom pods	4
Clove pods	4
Water	125 ml (4 fl oz / $\frac{1}{2}$ cup)

- Wash the rice and leave to soak for 1 hour.
- Marinate the chicken with the seasoning ingredients.
- Get ready a 20 x 30 x 5-cm (10 x 14 x 2-in) deep roasting tin or a casserole dish.
- Preheat the oven to 200°C (400°F).
- Arrange the chicken in a single layer in the roasting tin or casserole dish. Include all the seasoning.
- To partially cook the rice, assemble the rest of the ingredients for the rice (except the orange food colouring) in a pot or wok. Bring to a boil.
- In the meantime, drain the rice. Once the liquid comes to a boil, add the rice, lower the flame and put the cover on tightly. Let the rice cook over a low heat until the liquid is fully absorbed.

- Transfer the rice to the roasting tin or casserole dish. Spread the rice in an even layer over the chicken. Sprinkle the orange food colouring over the rice but do not mix it in or the rice grains will all be coloured an even light orange. We want only some of the rice grains to be bright and intensely orange, providing beautiful accents of colour in the presentation of the dish.
- Cover the baking or casserole dish tightly with foil. Seal all the edges well. Cook in the oven for 40 minutes. Leave the rice in the oven for another 15 minutes to complete the cooking.
- Remove the dish from the oven. Discard the foil. Sprinkle the rice with the fried shallots, roasted cashew nuts and coriander leaves. Serve.

braise

Braising or simmering is similar to steaming—it is a moist heat method, a much larger quantity of fluid is included, and the dish is covered so no moisture is lost. This method is well suited to cooking tough cuts of meat that have longer muscle fibres as well as more connective tissues. Long gentle cooking enables the collagen in the connective tissues to cook to a lovely gelatinous texture.

Occasionally, when braising on the stovetop, I have been blissfully unaware that the fire was too low to maintain a simmer. Sometimes, the flame was too big, causing the gravy to evaporate too fast or even to boil over. When you braise in the oven according to the right temperature and length of time, the food will be perfectly cooked without any fussing on your part. The long braising time frees you to do other food preparations or simply relax till it is time to eat.

The base of the pot does not come into direct contact with the heating element in the oven, as it surely does when braising on the stovetop. The heat in the oven is diffused and surrounds the pot of simmering ingredients gently. All these eliminate the risk of scorching the food at the bottom of the pot.

What can you braise in the oven? Seafood stews are better and more efficiently cooked on the stove as seafood cooks very quickly. Poultry, meat and vegetable stews are obvious choices. In short, any kind of food that requires a long simmering time can be cooked in the oven. If your oven is big enough, you can braise two dishes at the same time.

The cooking times for the recipes are estimates. They range from about 30 minutes to two hours. Numerous variables determine cooking time—the type and cut of meat or vegetables, the size and temperature of the ingredients when they enter the oven, the quantity of liquid, the amount of ingredients being cooked and the oven setting. The distance between the food and the heating elements of the particular oven is another factor that influences the speed of heat transfer. Sounds complicated? Braising in the oven is actually quite straightforward in practice. The good thing is that some extra minutes of cooking will not do any harm to the dish. Conversely, if something is undercooked, cooking time can be easily increased by a turn of the dial.

Long-cooking stews can be given a head start by bringing them to a full boil on the stovetop first. Using a low to medium stove flame will ensure that the liquid and ingredients, especially chunkier pieces of meat are well heated through before they go into the preheated oven. This step, together with the preheating of the oven, helps reduce cooking time, especially when cooking stews with more liquid. Occasionally I might start a dish on the stovetop by frying the aromatic ingredients like ginger, garlic or a spice paste, before adding all the other ingredients and then complete the cooking in the oven. When the dish is done, it is left in the oven (with the heat turned off) to keep warm till serving time.

Preheating is not necessary for some of the recipes in which the meat pieces are placed in a single layer in the baking dish with a small amount of liquid. This arrangement ensures that each piece of meat is getting a similar amount of heat at the same time.

I can't repeat often enough how useful the oven is for this moist heat method of cooking, especially when it is a dish that requires you to be checking and stirring intermittently for the duration of its cooking time on the stovetop. The oven eliminates all that. It is extremely reassuring to know that dinner is gently simmering in the oven and will be ready in an hour or two. In the meantime, all that is required of you is to cook the rice or some other dish to accompany it, wash up and leave your kitchen pristinely clean long before dinner is ready.

chicken in creamy coconut sauce *serves 4*

When you feel like making curry but are not up to grinding and frying spice mixtures, then this is the recipe I would recommend. It is what I call the fraternal twin to the ubiquitous curry chicken. Almost all the basic aromatic ingredients of curry chicken are there. You only need to slice them, assemble everything and pop the whole lot into the oven.

Chicken legs	4, about 200 g (7 oz) each, cut into 4 pieces each
Lemongrass	1 stalk, cut into 5-cm (2-in) lengths and crushed
Red chillies	2, seeded and sliced in half lengthwise
Bird's eye chilli	2, seeded
Shallots	6, peeled and sliced
Garlic	2, peeled and sliced
Bay leaves	3
Pandan leaves	2, tied into a knot
Coconut milk	250 ml (8 fl oz / 1 cup)
Water	180 ml (6 fl oz / $^3/_4$ cup)
Salt	$1^1/_4$ tsp
Sugar	1 tsp

- Preheat the oven to 200°C (400°F).

- Put all the ingredients in a pot and bring to a boil over a medium flame. Cover the pot and cook in the oven for 30 minutes.

- Serve with rice.

curry chicken, with ease *serves 4-6*

There are as many different versions and recipes for curry chicken as there are people who cook it. To all these wonderfully enticing variations of home-style, handed down recipes, there are the numerous commercially prepared curry pastes and powders to which only chicken, potatoes and coconut milk need to be added.

If you are averse to a know-it-all friend or relative openly declaring, "Oh, you used so-and-so curry powder, right?" Then this curry is the one for you. You'll be surprised to know that this recipe uses not one, but two commercially manufactured products. You may not be able to fool a curry chicken connoisseur with one product, but a combination of two would do it!

This is the curry my mother-in-law always cooks—one her grandchildren will always associate with her and remember her by. She enjoys cooking the Sunday dinner for the whole extended family. Her busy schedule (golf, mahjong, dancing) means simple uncomplicated food that can be prepared with ease. Hence this particular curry chicken is her piece de resistance at the table. She learned this recipe from her sister-in-law, Aunty Judy, who must be given full credit for coming up with this brilliant take on cooking curry.

This recipe is very amenable to tweaking. Add one or two turmeric leaves and you'll have what I call a Malay curry; a whole cut up lemongrass and some kaffir lime leaves will impart some Thai zing to it while a generous handful of curry leaves will infuse it with the flavour of Indian curries.

Preparation merely involves some peeling, cutting and mixing. There is no frying. All the ingredients are assembled and cooked. Coconut milk is added at the end and that's it.

Bottled sambal *belacan*	4 Tbsp
Meat or chicken curry powder	4 Tbsp
Water	180 ml (6 fl oz / 3/4 cup)
Salt	1 tsp
Chicken legs	4, about 200 g (7 oz) each, cut into 3 pieces each
Potatoes	2, medium, peeled and cut into 8 pieces each
Fragrant leaves	(1–2 turmeric leaves, 1 stalk lemongrass 3–4 kaffir lime leaves, a handful curry leaves)
Coconut milk	250 ml (8 fl oz / 1 cup), extracted from 1 grated coconut and sufficient water

- Put the sambal *belacan* and the curry powder directly into the pot you are using to cook the curry. Add 1–2 Tbsp water and mix to form a smooth paste. Add the remaining water and salt. Stir until curry paste is evenly mixed.

- Now add the chicken, potatoes and any fragrant leaves. Make sure the potatoes are immersed in the liquid to ensure proper cooking. It is all right if the liquid does not cover parts of the chicken.

- Preheat the oven set to 200°C (400°F).

- Bring the chicken to a boil over a small-medium flame on the stovetop. Cover the pot and cook in the oven for 30 minutes.

- Remove pot from the oven. Add coconut milk and stir through. Cover the pot and return it to the oven for another 5 minutes. Turn off the oven. You can leave the curry in the oven to keep warm until you are ready to serve.

- Serve with rice or bread.

emperor herbs chicken *serves 6*

As a child, when western medicine failed to cure my ailments, I was coerced to swallow an entire bowl of disgusting, nauseatingly bitter black liquid brewed from various types of Chinese herbs. It was pure unadulterated torture. Mind you it was a whole bowl, as opposed to a teaspoonful or two of cough syrup or antihistamine. I have sworn off anything remotely herbal that has invaded the culinary domain—including ginseng soups or any other supposedly health-inducing tonic concoctions.

I finally conceded after repeated persuasions by my mom and sisters (who had gone through the same ordeal) to try this particular herbal chicken, cooked with packaged spices. My initial reservations gave way to pleasant surprise. It was actually quite good and tasted nothing like those vile medicinal brews.

Since that first taste, I have cooked this dish several times. My mom steams this chicken for about an hour although the instructions on the packet suggest a steaming time of two-and-a-half hours! Of course I prefer steaming it in the oven, saving myself the repeated task of topping up the water in the steamer. It also takes only a fraction of the suggested cooking time.

Chicken legs	4, about 200 g (7 oz) each, thighs and drumsticks separated, skinned if desired
Store-bought herbal chicken spices	1 packet
Chinese wolfberries	1 Tbsp
Chinese red dates	12, pitted
Water	4 Tbsp
Light soy sauce	2 Tbsp
Sesame oil	2 tsp

- Arrange chicken pieces in a casserole dish in a single layer. Sprinkle the herbal chicken spices over and coat each piece completely with the marinade. Leave to marinate for about 30 minutes. The chicken pieces must be at room temperature when they go into the oven.

- Just before cooking, add wolfberries, red dates, water and light soy sauce to the dish. Cover tightly with foil and cook in the oven set to 200°C (400°F) for 45 minutes. There is no need to preheat the oven.

- Drizzle sesame oil over the chicken just before serving.

chicken braised in essence of chicken *serves 4–6*

Essence of chicken is reputed to have extensive health benefits, from relieving exhaustion to reducing blood sugar levels. But not everyone is partial to its taste. I quite enjoy it though—its natural umami flavour is a definite plus factor when used as an ingredient in chicken dishes. I came across a brief write-up of this dish in a newspaper review of a restaurant. The reviewer raved about this dish so much I just had to cook it. Based on the few ingredients he mentioned—mushrooms, chicken and of course, essence of chicken, I concocted my own version here.

Chicken legs	4, about 200 g (7 oz) each, cut into 4 pieces and skinned if desired
Chinese wolfberries	1 Tbsp
Essence of chicken	2 bottles
Light soy sauce	1 Tbsp
Salt	1/4 tsp
Dried Chinese mushrooms	6, rinsed and soaked to soften
Garlic	2 cloves, peeled and sliced
Ginger	2 slices

- Preheat the oven to 200°C (400°F).

- Arrange chicken pieces in a single layer in a casserole dish. Scatter wolfberries over the chicken.

- Stir essence of chicken, light soy sauce and salt together. Pour this over the chicken.

- Remove the mushrooms from the soaking water without squeezing out any liquid. Tuck the mushrooms, garlic and ginger slices among the chicken pieces.

- Cover the dish tightly with foil and cook in the oven for 45 minutes. This dish can also be prepared in a claypot, but the oven temperature must be increased to 220°C (425°F) and the cooking time to 1 hour if your claypot cannot accomodate the chicken in a single layer.

butter chicken *serves 5–6*

This recipe for butter chicken was given to me by my friend, Bansoor Kaur. And what a lovely dish this is—aromatic and creamy, with a light tang from the tomatoes cutting through the richness. The original recipe calls for 125 g (4¼ oz) butter, on top of almost a cup of cream! Eaten with garlic-butter and cheese naan (page 142), it makes for such an indulgent meal. This dish also goes fabulously well with pilaf.

I have made some changes to Bansoor's recipe. The butter is reduced to 60 g (2 oz). The chicken is skinned to avoid an overload of saturated fats. I also conveniently use a can of tomato puree as opposed to blanching tomatoes, skinning and pureeing them myself. Canned tomato puree comes in varying degrees of thickness. In this recipe, I use 300 ml (10 fl oz / 1¼ cups) thick tomato puree with the addition of 125 ml (4 fl oz / ½ cup) water. If using a thinner puree, increase the puree to 435 ml (14 fl oz / 1¾ cups) and leave out the water.

Chicken	1, about 1.2 kg (2 lb 6 oz)
Butter	60 g (2 oz)
Ginger	2 large thumb-size knobs, peeled and finely grated to get 4 Tbsp grated ginger and juice
Garlic	8 cloves, peeled and finely grated
Green chillies	4, seeded
Cinnamon sticks	2
Cardamoms	10
Chilli powder	2 tsp
Tomato puree	300 ml (10 fl oz / 1¼ cups)
Water	125 ml (4 fl oz / ½ cup)
Sugar	1½ Tbsp
Salt	1¾ tsp
Heavy (double) cream (at least 30% fat)	180 ml (6 fl oz / ¾ cup)

- Get a pot with a cover ready. A cast iron or stainless steel one is good for this recipe.

- Separate the chicken into wings, drumsticks, thighs and breast. Cut the breast in half along one side of the breastbone. You will end up with 8 parts, including the wings. Freeze the backbone and neck for making stock for other recipes. Remove chicken skin if desired.

- Melt butter in the pot over a small to medium flame. Sauté ginger, garlic, cinnamon sticks and cardamoms in the butter. When the ginger and garlic start to brown, add chilli powder. Stir for a few seconds before adding the chicken. Increase the flame to medium and mix the chicken well with the aromatic ingredients.

- In the meantime, preheat the oven to 170°C (338°F).

- Stir in tomato puree, coating the chicken pieces well. Use the water to rinse out the tomato can and add this to the mixture in the pot. Include the sugar and salt. Slowly bring the dish to a full boil.

- When the chicken comes to a boil, cover the pot and cook this in the oven for 40 minutes.

- At the end of the 40 minutes, stir in the cream. Return the pot to the oven for another 5 minutes at 200°C (400°F). Leave in the oven to keep warm until ready to serve.

dhal curry *serves 4*

I usually cook this dhal curry together with the butter chicken (page 52) as my oven can accommodate both pots comfortably. The dhal cooks faster than the chicken, but it won't be hurt by a few minutes of extra cooking.

There are different varieties of dhal, also known as lentils. They come in various colours—yellow, orange, green and brown. I use Masoor lentils, which are smaller and hence soften faster.

Vegetables like aubergines, ladies fingers and tomatoes can be added to the dhal and cooked together till soft. This dish is suitable for lacto-vegetarians. Serve this with the garlic-butter and cheese naan (page 142).

Dhal	135 g (4$^3/_4$ oz)
Curry leaves	2 stalks
Cooking oil	1 Tbsp
Mustard seeds	1 tsp
Cumin seeds	$^1/_2$ tsp
Green chillies	2, seeded and cut in half
Chilli powder	1 tsp
Turmeric powder	$^1/_2$ tsp
Water	625–750 ml (20–24 fl oz / 2$^1/_2$–3 cups)
Salt	1$^1/_4$–1$^1/_2$ tsp

- Wash the dhal and soak in water for 1 hour.

- Wash the curry leaves and dry thoroughly on kitchen towels.

- Preheat the oven to 150°C (300°F). Drain the dhal and discard the soaking water.

- Heat the oil in a medium pot over a small flame. When the oil is hot, add mustard and cumin seeds. They will sizzle and start spluttering after a few seconds. Stir and allow for a few more seconds of spluttering before adding the curry leaves. Simply strip the leaves off the stalk into the pot. The leaves will sizzle immediately. Stir that around for a couple more seconds and transfer half of the seeds and leaves to a small dish. This will be used as a garnish later on.

- Add the green chillies, chilli and turmeric powders to the content in the pot. Fry for a couple of seconds and then add all the drained dhal. Add 625 ml (20 fl oz / 2$^1/_2$ cups) water for a thicker curry or 750 ml (24 fl oz / 3 cups) of water for a thinner one. Add the salt according to the amount of water added. Let everything come to a boil.

- Cover the pot and transfer the dhal to the oven. Cook for 30 minutes or up to 45 minutes if you like the dhal soft to the point of disintegration.

- When the dhal is cooked, give it a stir and check the seasoning, adding more salt as necessary. Let the dhal sit in the oven to keep warm. Add the reserved fried seeds and curry leaves before serving.

green curry with chicken *serves 4–6*

Chicken curry—whether it's the Chinese, Malay or Indian version—has a lovely warm orange hue with an appealing layer of bright orange-red chilli oil on top. Having grown accustomed to this palette, it was somewhat disconcerting the first time I sampled green curry. Even a lifetime of curry-eating did nothing to prepare me for the unusual unfathomable taste of that first mouthful. No single ingredient stood out wrestling for dominance. It was a perfect blend of all those herbs and spices used in its making—like a tight a cappella piece, the whole is more than the sum of its parts.

It was a surprise to find that green curry shares many similar ingredients with our familiar curries, just with the addition of green items like green chillies, coriander leaves and kaffir lime leaves. It is so good eaten with pineapple rice.

Lemongrass	1 stalk
Kaffir lime leaves	8
Shallots	4, peeled
Garlic	2 cloves, peeled
Green bird's eye chilli	6, seeded
Galangal	1 thumb-size knob, peeled and thinly sliced
Coriander leaves (cilantro)	1 large stalk, roughly chopped
Dried prawn (shrimp) paste (*belacan*)	1 tsp
Coconut milk	250 ml (8 fl oz / 1 cup)
Ground white pepper	1 tsp
Coriander powder	1 tsp
Cumin powder	1/2 tsp
Water	125 ml (4 fl oz / 1/2 cup)
Fish sauce	3 Tbsp
Sugar	2 tsp
Chicken legs	4, about 200 g (7 oz) each, cut into 4 pieces each and skinned if desired
Aubergine (eggplant /brinjal)	1, about 200 g (7 oz), cut into wedges

- Cut off 5-cm (2-in) from the root end of the lemongrass and thinly slice this. Keep the rest of the lemongrass to be added to the curry later. Cut off and discard the central veins of 4 kaffir lime leaves. Combine shallots, garlic, lemongrass root, galangal, coriander and kaffir lime leaves in a blender and blend until smooth.

- Add dried prawn paste and coconut milk, and blend until well combined. The coconut milk may curdle but don't let that alarm you. It won't matter one bit.

- Pour the blended ingredients into a pot. Stir in pepper, coriander and cumin powders, water, fish sauce and sugar.

- Preheat the oven to 200°C (400°F).

- Put chicken and the remaining kaffir lime leaves into the pot. Bring everything to a boil over a small flame.

- When the curry comes to a boil, place the aubergine pieces on top. It doesn't matter that the aubergine pieces are not immersed in the curry at this stage. Cover the pot and put it in the oven. Cook for 30 minutes.

- When the curry is done, stir the aubergine into it. Taste and adjust seasoning as needed.

braised pork in dark soy sauce loh bak *serves 8–10*

The axiom *familiarity breeds contempt* does not apply to this old familiar dish of braised pork that has been cooked in practically every Chinese kitchen for generations. The deep reassuring flavours of the braised pork belie the simplicity of its preparation. Porridge or rice, generously smothered with the savoury sauce, is for many the keystone of comforting home cooked food.

I wasn't particularly fond of this dish as a child. But as I grow older, I find myself cooking this braised pork more frequently than I expected. Perhaps with the increase in age comes an ever-deepening desire to return to my culinary roots.

You may think 875 ml (28 fl oz / 3^1/$_2$ cups) water in the ingredient list too much. But you must know that my mama always cooks this dish with lots of sauce. The leftover sauce will be used to braise a head of cabbage or she would break a few eggs into the sauce, stir the eggs and sauce together, then cook gently until the eggs set to a lovely soft consistency—Asian scrambled eggs.

Pork belly is the cut used ubiquitously in this dish. You can substitute with pork shoulder if you prefer a higher lean meat to fat ratio.

Pork belly or shoulder	4 strips, about 1 kg (2 lb 3 oz)
Water	875 ml (28 fl oz / 3^1/$_2$ cups)
Superior dark soy sauce	3 Tbsp
Salt	1^1/$_2$ tsp
Ground white pepper	^{1}/$_4$ tsp
Oyster sauce	1 Tbsp
Garlic	10 cloves, peeled and crushed
Hard-boiled eggs	8, shelled
Corn flour (cornstarch)	3 Tbsp, mixed with 125 ml (4 fl oz / ^{1}/$_2$ cup) water

- Wash the pork and drain well. Use a pair of tweezers to remove any hair from the skin.

- Put water, dark soy sauce, salt, pepper and oyster sauce into a pot. Stir to mix well. Add pork, garlic and eggs. Put the pot on the stove and bring to a boil over a medium flame.

- Meanwhile, preheat the oven to 150°C (300°F).

- When the pork starts to come to a boil, add corn flour mixture and stir well. Let everything come to a boil again to cook the corn flour. Turn off the flame. Put the lid on and transfer the whole pot to the oven to cook for 1 hour 30 minutes.

- After the first hour, you may want to check and turn any pieces of pork or egg that is not completely submerged in the sauce.

- When the pork has braised for the full 1 hour 30 minutes, just leave it in the oven (with the heat turned off) until you are ready to eat.

- To serve, slice the pork into pieces, and the eggs into wedges. Arrange on a serving plate and pour the sauce over.

beef and radish stew *serves 4*

How often is it when a planned menu of beef stew is foiled by the absence of lacy fats in the stewing beef at the meat counter? Those lean cuts will not transform into meat that just melts in your mouth. On the other hand, when the beef is intricately marbled with fats, it is almost criminal to pass it up and adhere to my meticulously thought out menu. Beef stew is one of our family favourites. It is the sort of heart-warming thing to eat that makes one feel comforted, satisfied and satiated.

There are several cuts of beef that work marvellously in a stew. They are the brisket, shin and short ribs. The common denominator among them is the fats that give the cooked meat its moist, melting texture. The long braising process turns the tough connective tissues of the meat into soluble gelatine that adds to the tenderness of the meat.

Almost every Asian country has its own version of beef stew seasoned with iconic ingredients. Japanese beef stew with sake and mirin and Vietnamese stew with lemongrass and fish sauce are just two examples. The popular *ngau nnam meen* (beef brisket noodles) is a lovely dish of brisket simmered in gravy infused with spices like star anise and then served with noodles. Even beef *rendang* with its complex flavours derived from the use of numerous herbs and spices, is a type of stew.

Additions to stews usually come in the form of root vegetables which also need gentle cooking to reach a soft tender state. Carrots, potatoes and radishes are popular choices. It might be a good idea to rotate the inclusion of these vegetables, or use a different combination each time to keep things interesting. For this particular recipe, I have chosen radish. It imparts a certain sweetness to the stew and at the same time absorbs the flavour of the braising liquid.

This stew is good served with bread, plain rice, or even better, with buttered rice.

Beef brisket (well-marbled)	500 g (1 lb 1½ oz), cut into 2-cm (1-in) cubes
Carrot	1, about 150 g (5 oz), peeled and cut into bite-size chunks
Radish	½, about 150 g (5 oz), peeled and cut into bite-size chunks
Onion	1 large, peeled and cut into wedges
Garlic	4 cloves, peeled and crushed
Light soy sauce	2 Tbsp
Oyster sauce	½ Tbsp
Water	250 ml (8 fl oz / 1 cup)
Ground white pepper	¼ tsp
Coriander leaves (cilantro)	1 stalk, chopped

- Put the beef, carrot, radish, onion and garlic into a pot. Mix in light soy sauce, oyster sauce, water and pepper.

- Preheat the oven to 150°C (300°F).

- Bring the ingredients to a roaring boil over a small to medium fire.

- Put the lid on tightly and cook in the oven for 2 hours.

- Taste and adjust seasoning to taste. Garnish with the coriander leaves.

korean ginseng chicken sam-gye-tang *serves 4*

My vehement dislike of anything herbal stopped me from trying out this dish for many years. This resistance was further intensified by the taste of a vacuumed package of *sam-gye-tang* that my sister-in-law bought in Korea. I won't try to describe for you what that tasted like, except to say that it wasn't anything I imagined *sam-gye-tang* to be like—it was quite inedible.

My mom loves ginseng, always has. Her generation and those before have been brought up to revere Chinese herbs as well as to propagate their medicinal and health benefits. *Sam-gye-tang* was a dish my mom had always wanted to try cooking but never got down to it.

When it struck me that *sam-gye-tang* is perfectly suited to being cooked in the oven, I finally decided to give it a shot. To mitigate the strong taste of the ginseng, I used only one ginseng root which was added to the water. The soup was actually good, with only the barest hint of ginseng. The glutinous rice was delicious, infused with the fragrance of garlic and plump with the chicken juices. For a stronger ginseng flavour, use two to three ginseng roots.

You need an ovenproof pot that the chicken can snugly fit into. I wish I could include more glutinous rice but the 1/2 cup of rice is just right. The rice will swell during cooking and fill up the cavity of the chicken. There is a disproportionate amount of chicken to the soup but adding more water will dilute the soup. If you want to increase the amount of soup, I suggest you add chicken stock and an extra ginseng root to bolster the full flavour of this soup.

Glutinous rice	90 g (3 oz)
Whole chicken	1, about 1 kg (2 lb 3 oz)
Water	1 litre (32 fl oz / 4 cups)
Salt	1/4 tsp + more to taste
Garlic	10 cloves, peeled
Red dates	10, pitted
Ginseng roots	1–2
Ground white pepper	to taste
Spring onion (scallion) (optional)	1, finely sliced

- Wash the glutinous rice and soak in water for 1 hour.

- Wash the chicken well, drain it and place it in an ovenproof pot. The chicken must be at room temperature.

- Put 1 litre (32 fl oz / 4 cups) of water into another pot and bring to a boil. Or you can just boil water using a kettle.

- Preheat the oven to 220°C (425°F).

- Drain the soaked rice and season with 1/4 tsp salt. Stuff the rice into the cavity of the chicken together with 3–4 cloves of garlic, a similar number of red dates and a ginseng root. Close the cavity by overlapping the skin and secure with a toothpick. Put the chicken into the pot with the breast side up.

- Pour the boiling water into the pot. The water should almost cover the chicken. Add the remaining garlic, red dates and ginseng to the water. Cover the pot tightly and cook in the oven for 45 minutes.

- Bring the pot out of the oven. Turn the chicken over carefully, cover and return to the oven. Cook for a further 15 minutes. Season with salt and pepper to taste.

- To serve, ladle the soup into bowls. Cut the chicken along the breastbone with a pair of kitchen scissors. Try to keep the glutinous rice intact. Using a spoon, scoop a big lump of the rice and place into each bowl. Cut the chicken into smaller pieces and place a piece in each bowl. Garnish with spring onion if desired.

braised preserved mustard greens mei cai *serves 5–6*

This is a dish I didn't enjoy in my younger days. The dark colours and the fatty pork turned me off. My younger son loves it and my mama was pleasantly surprised.

The preserved mustard greens (*mei cai*) need to be thoroughly washed. Mama's tip is to cut up the vegetables into smaller pieces and wash them in a big pot or basin filled with water. She shakes the vegetables thoroughly in the water to loosen the grit and soil, which will sink to the bottom. She then squeezes the vegetables, handful by handful, really dry and transfers them to a bowl. The whole process is repeated about three to four times till the water is clear and there is no more sand at the bottom of the pot. The vegetables are then left to soak for an hour.

Preserved mustard greens love the oil that is rendered by the fatty pork during the cooking process. The oil lubricates the vegetables, giving them a smooth and luxurious feel in the mouth.

Mama has two methods of cooking this dish, the first one being more labour intensive. The pieces of pork belly are marinated and fried with oil and garlic first, then set aside. The vegetables are fried next with a bit more oil and garlic. Vegetables and meat are then layered in a bowl and steamed for about an hour and a half till the meat is tender. The second method is to omit the frying, put everything into a pot and braise the whole lot on the stove.

I can understand the frying which delivers an extra fragrance to the dish. But steaming is too much of a chore (topping up the water repeatedly) for a dish as simple as this.

Braising this dish in the oven makes perfect sense. It frees me from the stirring and checking to make sure the small flame is not extinguished by an unexpected breeze, or the liquid is not evaporating too fast, or that the contents of the pot does not boil over. The correct temperature and time set for the oven will ensure that the food is cooked just right without all of the above concerns.

Mama uses both sweet and salty preserved mustard greens. That is what I have done here, using equal amounts of each type, which I think makes for the best combination.

Sweet preserved mustard greens	200 g (7 oz)
Salty preserved mustard greens	200 g (7 oz)
Pork belly	400 g (14 oz)
Garlic	6–8 cloves, peeled
Dark soy sauce	1 Tbsp
Oyster sauce	1 tsp
Water	375 ml (12 fl oz / 1¹/₂ cups)

- Cut up the sweet and salty preserved mustard greens into smaller pieces. A pair of kitchen scissors is excellent for this. Put the vegetables in a big pot filled with water. Shake the vegetables vigorously to loosen the grit and soil. Squeeze the vegetables very dry, one handful at a time and transfer to a colander or bowl. Repeat the washing process a few times until the water is clear and there is no more grit at the bottom. Now soak the vegetables for 1 hour.

- Cut up the pork belly into fairly big chunks. The fat will become so tender later that if you cut the pieces too small, the meat will break up easily. Mash the garlic by whacking each clove with a knife. Marinate the pork belly with

the garlic, dark soy sauce and oyster sauce in an ovenproof pot with a lid. Stoneware or cast iron pots are excellent. Do not omit the oyster sauce—that 1 tsp helps to round up the flavour of the dish.

- Squeeze the vegetables dry once again and put them into the pot with the meat. Add the water. Turn on the oven to 150°C (300°F). Bring the meat and vegetables to a boil over a medium flame. Now put the covered pot into the oven and cook for 1 hour 30 minutes.

braised mushrooms with dried scallops *serves 4–6*

This is a very versatile mushroom stew to which you can add any variety of other ingredients like sea cucumber, chicken, dried oysters, *fatt choy* (literally hair vegetable), and even abalone.

You can use cute little dried Chinese mushrooms that will expand to bite-size pieces when hydrated. Bigger mushrooms just need to be cut up after hydrating. I use the small dried scallops—inexpensive, yet flavourful and they do not require soaking.

The braised mushrooms can be cooked a day in advance and reheated before serving. In fact it tastes better the day after. The mushrooms can be served in a big bowl lined with Chinese or iceberg lettuce.

Cooking oil	1^1/$_2$ Tbsp
Shallots	4, peeled and sliced
Garlic	4 cloves, peeled and minced
Dried Chinese mushrooms	50 g (2 oz), soaked to soften
Button mushrooms	1 can, about 450 g (1 lb), drained
Straw mushrooms	1 can, about 450 g (1 lb), drained
Water	375 ml (12 fl oz / 1^1/$_2$ cups)
Dried scallops	50 g (2 oz), rinsed
Oyster sauce	1^1/$_2$ Tbsp
Chinese cooking wine (Shaoxing)	1 Tbsp
Dark soy sauce	^{1}/$_2$ tsp
Sugar	^{1}/$_2$ tsp
Corn flour (cornstarch)	2 tsp
Sesame oil	^{1}/$_2$ tsp
Ground white pepper	to taste

- Heat oil in a pot and fry the sliced shallots. When the shallots start to brown, add the garlic. Fry until garlic turns golden brown. Toss in all the mushrooms and stir well.

- Add 300 ml (10 fl oz / 1^1/$_4$ cups) water. Now include the dried scallops, oyster sauce, wine, dark soy sauce and sugar. Stir well and bring to a boil.

- Stir the corn flour with the remaining water. Add this to the pot, stirring continuously for a few seconds.

- Cover the pot and transfer to the oven. Cook for 30 minutes. Check the seasoning. The dried scallops impart a fair bit of salinity to the gravy hence additional salt may not be needed.

- If you are serving immediately, bring the pot of mushrooms out and stir in the sesame oil and a few dashes of pepper. Or leave the mushrooms to keep warm in the oven, adding the sesame oil and pepper just before serving.

green bean soup *serves 4-6*

This ubiquitous but well-loved sweet soup is often eaten as a snack or dessert. In the gentle diffused heat of the oven, the beans cook to a lovely tenderness and yet hold their shape well. There is little separation of the beans from the seed coats—a pleasant surprise the first time I cooked this in the oven.

Green beans	180 g (6$\frac{1}{3}$ oz)
Water	1.5 litres (48 fl oz / 6 cups)
Coconut milk	125 ml (4 fl oz / $\frac{1}{2}$ cup)
Sugar	112 g (4 oz) or more to taste
Pandan leaves	2, washed and knotted
Sago pearls	2 Tbsp

- Wash the beans and soak in water for 1 hour.

- Drain the beans, discarding the water.

- Preheat the oven to 160°C (325°F).

- Put the beans, water, coconut milk, sugar and pandan leaves into a pot. Place the pot over a small-medium flame until the contents come to a boil. Taste for sweetness, adding more sugar if needed. Cover the pot and transfer to the oven. Cook for 30 minutes.

- Stir in sago. Continue to cook, covered for another 15 minutes. Leave the soup in the oven (with the heat turned off) to keep warm before serving.

black rice porridge pulot hitam *serves 4–6*

Like green bean soup, black rice porridge can be a snack or dessert, depending on when it is served. The name itself, both exotic and mysterious, is enough to tantalise anyone to try it. Surprisingly the rice is not black as one would assume. It is actually a deep shade of purple-black with a hint of maroon. The water in which the rice is cooked in will be imbued with its beautiful rich hue.

If the oven can accommodate, this or the green bean soup (page 68) can share oven space with a meat stew—and there you have it: the main course and dessert.

Black glutinous rice	100 g (3^1/$_2$ oz)
Water	1.5 litres (48 fl oz / 6 cups)
Sugar	112 g (4 oz)
Salt	^{1}/$_2$ tsp
Pandan leaves	2, washed and knotted
Corn flour (cornstarch)	4 Tbsp, mixed with 4 Tbsp water
Coconut milk	125 ml (4 fl oz / ^{1}/$_2$ cup)

- Wash the rice and leave to soak overnight in the fridge.

- Preheat the oven to 150°C (300°F).

- Drain the rice. Assemble rice, water, sugar, salt and pandan leaves in a pot. Bring to a roaring boil over a small-medium flame.

- Cover the pot tightly. Transfer to the oven and cook for 1 hour 15 minutes.

- Stir corn flour mixture into the black rice porridge after the initial cooking time. Resume cooking with the lid on for another 15 minutes.

- Remove from the oven, taste and add more sugar if needed. Serve immediately or return the pot to the oven to keep warm.

- To serve, ladle into bowls and drizzle coconut milk over.

fry

There are four frying methods—dry-frying, stir-frying, shallow-frying and deep-frying. Let's look at each in turn and see whether these methods can be adapted to the oven.

Dry-frying

This is the method used for frying spices (like peppercorns) to intensify flavours. There is no oil needed, that is why it is "dry". It is more convenient to fry small quantities of spices on the stovetop as they fry very quickly.

When dry-frying a large amount, say a few hundred grammes of peppercorns on the stove, it is necessary to stand by the stove and stir the lot frequently to ensure even heating. The spices at the bottom of the wok or pot will get hot very much faster as they are separated from the flame by the mere thickness of the wok or pot.

It is more convenient to dry-fry large amounts of spices in the oven. The spices can be spread in a thin layer on a tray. This allows the spices to get a fairly equal distribution of heat from the bottom and top of the oven. Stirring the spices once midway is all that is needed. At a temperature of 200°C (400°F), it would take about 10 minutes for the spices to be heated through thoroughly.

Food that is inherently fatty can also be dry-fried as there is no need for extra oil to be added. Bacon and tuna belly exude their own fats when fried, whether on the stove or in the oven. To replicate this method in the oven, simply place pieces of these items on a tray and pop the lot into the oven. They will be fried in their own fat. You only need to turn the pieces over midway during cooking time for more even browning.

Stir-frying

In stir-frying, a hot roaring fire produces the intense heat to cook the food. The food must be constantly stirred. Sometimes a bit of liquid is added to quickly braise the food. As the ingredients are cut into bite-size pieces, they can be cooked in a very short time. Stir-frying is a fast, exciting, hands-on method of cooking, which unfortunately cannot be replicated in the oven.

The oven, even at its highest setting, cannot generate the kind of heat needed for stir-frying. On top of that, the stirring (not "staring", as Martin Yan likes to say) can only be done with the oven door open. You can visualise how ridiculous it is to attempt stir-frying in the oven.

Shallow-frying

Shallow-frying requires a thin layer of oil in which food is fried. This method is typically used to fry fish and flat pieces of meat; pork chops and chicken chops can be fried in this manner. The food absorbs some of the oil as it fries. It browns nicely and forms a scrumptious crust, which is the objective of frying.

Shallow-frying can be done in the oven. But only certain types of meat and vegetables are suitable for this particular method. Let me explain.

When shallow-frying on the stove, the ingredients are in very close proximity to the fire, separated only by the thickness of the frying pan. This allows the food to brown very quickly on the outside as the heat travels to the centre of the food to cook the entire piece. Hence thin pieces of pork chop will not get overcooked to the point of dry cardboard while its exterior crisps. In the oven, that distance between the heat source and the food is increased numerous times. Hence a longer time is required for the food to brown adequately. All of which means you cannot oven-fry seafood or thin slices of meat. They would be dry and overcooked by the time their exterior browns sufficiently.

Any meat to be fried has to be in fairly large or thick pieces, and must be able to withstand a longer cooking time to achieve the browning without drying up. Chicken legs (with or without bones) are the most suitable cuts. When fried with the skin on, there is no need for any additional oil. The skin will exude more than enough fat to fry the chicken. The leg meat also contains more intra-muscular fat, which helps to keep the meat moist during the longer cooking time. This means that you can fry boneless chicken chops or bone-in chicken pieces in the oven. Breaded chicken chops fry equally well as long as each piece of chicken is brushed with oil first to help the breadcrumbs adhere to it.

To further ensure that the meat is not overcooked by the time its outside browns, the meat should be well chilled when it goes into the oven. The heat then takes longer to penetrate into the centre of the meat, hence buying time for the outside to crisp.

What about vegetables? Can they be shallow-fried in the oven? Root vegetables take well to being cooked in the oven. In western cuisine, vegetables like potatoes and carrots are tossed with oil and roasted. Without splitting hairs over the technicality of the terms "roast" and "fry", I'll use the latter to describe food (meat or vegetable) that is coated with fat and cooked in the dry heat of the oven. You can call it "oven-fry" if it makes you happier.

Deep-frying

Deep-frying is cooking food immersed in a large amount of oil. Before you start imagining a huge pot of bubbling oil in the oven, let me assure you that neither a pot nor a large amount of oil is involved.

Like shallow-frying, food is deep-fried in considerably hot oil till the outside crisps and the inside is done. The difference between the two methods is the amount of oil involved.

In the oven however, the distinction between shallow- and deep-frying does not exist. First of all, the type of meat that can be fried in the oven is the same—it has to be of considerable thickness to withstand a longer cooking time so that exterior browning can occur without overcooking. Once again, chicken leg meat is a choice cut for this method. Secondly, the meat provides its own fats. Chicken wings are a case in point. They have a high fat to meat ratio, which makes them ideal to being fried in the oven without the addition of oil.

Frying a single tray of wings at one time gives the best browning results. The wings need to be turned once midway during cooking for more uniform browning. My 56-litre capacity built-in oven can fit in two trays of chicken wings—a total of about 18 to 20 wings (2 kg in weight). This opens the possibility of using two different marinades for the wings that can be ready in 30 minutes. They won't have the uniform brown of deep-fried wings. But what is that compared to being chained to the stove and frying batch after batch of wings? By the way, washing up is a cinch when you line the trays properly with aluminium foil which you will discard later.

Try out the recipes in this section and discover how easy it is to fry in the oven.

oven-fried prawn paste chicken wings ha cheong kai *serves 4*

Deep-frying food always prompts this question—what do you do with the oil after frying? Do you reuse it? I don't but there are definitely others who do. That pot of hot oil must be cooled, strained into a smaller container and kept in the fridge till the next time it is needed. All a bit bothersome, don't you think?

Oven-frying the chicken wings does not require additional oil as the skin will exude more than enough oil to fry the wings. There will even be oil left over on your baking tray. You won't have to wash the trays if they are properly lined with foil—another plus for oven-frying.

Cooking the wings one tray at a time (middle rack position) delivers the best browning results. If your oven can accommodate two trays simultaneously, it would save you time and energy. You will not need to switch tray positions midway through the roasting, but you'll have to turn the wings over for more effective browning.

You can oven-fry whole chicken wings, mid-joint wings or drummettes. Don't omit the corn flour. It helps to absorb the juices released by the chicken as it cooks. You can't substitute with plain flour, which becomes clumpy and unmanageable when mixed with the prawn paste and water. Corn flour will give a smooth and thin batter that coats the chicken nicely. The addition of some water to the marinade is only needed if the corn flour cakes, but include just enough to form a smooth marinade that coats the chicken well.

Chicken wings	1 kg (2 lb 3 oz)
Prawn (shrimp) paste (*ha cheong*)	1^1/$_2$ Tbsp
Water	1 Tbsp or more as needed
Corn flour (cornstarch)	2–4 Tbsp

- Wash chicken wings and drain them really well. Excess water will result in a very liquid marinade that pools at the bottom of whatever container you choose to marinate the wings in.

- Put the wings in a mixing bowl or pot. Add the prawn paste, water and 2 Tbsp corn flour. Mix well to coat each wing. If the marinade coats the wings well, there is no need to add more corn flour. Cover tightly and leave in the fridge to chill. This part of the preparation can be done a day in advance.

- To cook the wings, preheat the oven to 240°C (475°F) or 220°C (425°F) for a fan-assisted oven. Line a baking tray with foil and non-stick baking paper.

- Take the wings out of the fridge. Give them a final toss to ensure that they are evenly coated. Arrange them on the lined tray, spaced slightly apart. When the oven has reached the desired temperature, cook the wings in the oven for 15 minutes. Take the tray out and turn the wings over. Return them to the oven and cook another 15 minutes.

- Transfer the wings to a serving plate. Serve while they are hot and crispy.

garlicky honey wings *serves 4*

Honey wings make great finger food. For this reason, I prefer the mid-joint wings or drummettes. There may seem to be a copious amount of garlic in the recipe, but that is the whole point. Sweet, savoury and garlicky is what we're aiming for here. Do not be tempted to mix the honey together with the other seasonings when you marinate the wings. This will only result in burnt wings, as the honey will caramelise very quickly, after which it will start to burn long before the wings are done.

Chicken drummettes or mid-joint wings	1 kg (2 lb 3 oz)
Garlic	4–6 cloves, peeled and finely grated
Salt	$1^1/_4$ tsp
Ground black pepper	1 tsp
Corn flour (cornstarch)	4 Tbsp
Water	1 Tbsp, or as needed
Honey	125 ml (4 fl oz / $^1/_2$ cup)
Lime or lemon (optional)	to garnish

- Wash and drain chicken very well. Put the chicken, garlic, salt, pepper and corn flour in a mixing bowl or pot. Mix well to coat the chicken properly. Add a bit of water if the corn flour cakes. Cover the chicken and leave in the fridge to chill for at least 2 hours or overnight.

- Preheat the oven to 240°C (475°F) or 220°C (425°F) for a fan-assisted oven.

- Line a tray with foil and non-stick baking paper. Take the chicken out of the fridge. Toss them well one more time to ensure even coating of the marinade. Arrange the chicken, slightly spaced apart on the lined tray. Put the chicken in the oven to roast for 15 minutes. Take the tray out and turn the chicken over. Return to the oven and roast for another 10–15 minutes.

- Take the chicken out. Brush each drummette/wing (generously) with honey. Transfer the chicken to a plate and serve with the wedges of lime or lemon.

spicy crispy wings *serves 4*

These wings are like curry chicken wings, only better. Allow time for the flavour of the marinade to permeate into the chicken skin before frying in the oven. These wings are also excellent as finger food. You can use whole chicken wings, drummettes or mid-joint cuts.

Chicken wings	1 kg (2 lb 3 oz)
Corn flour (cornstarch)	2–3 Tbsp
Garlic	2 cloves, peeled and finely grated
Red bird's eye chilli	2–4, seeded and finely minced
Meat or chicken curry powder	2 Tbsp
Turmeric powder	2 tsp
Prawn (shrimp) paste (*ha cheong*)	$^1/_2$ Tbsp
Salt	$^3/_4$ tsp

- Wash and drain chicken wings well. Put all the ingredients into a mixing bowl adding just 2 Tbsp corn flour. Mix everything well to coat the wings with the marinade. Add an extra $^1/_2$–1 Tbsp corn flour only if the marinade is watery and pools to the bottom of the mixing bowl. We want a batter that is thick enough to coat the wings but not so thick that it cakes. Conversely, if the marinade is too dry, add a bit of water. Cover the wings and chill for at least 2 hours.

- Preheat the oven to 240°C (475°F) or 220°C (425°F) for a fan-assisted oven.

- Line a baking tray with foil and non-stick baking paper.

- Arrange the wings on the tray, spacing them slightly apart. Roast in the oven for 15 minutes. Take the tray out and turn the wings over. Roast for another 15 minutes.

- Transfer the wings to a serving plate and serve immediately.

fried chicken with garlic-soy sauce *serves 4*

Since the Korean wave hit Singapore almost a decade ago, all things Korean have become increasingly popular. From fashion to food, Korean culture is here to stay. It is hardly surprising that Korean fried chicken has found ready fans among a nation of fried chicken lovers.

Korean fried chicken is fried twice to attain that exterior crispiness before being coated with either a sweet sticky garlic-soy or a sweet-chilli sauce. In adapting this recipe to the oven, the wings once again are fried in their own fat. They are not as crispy as the twice-fried ones. But then again, the labour in preparing them is significantly reduced, and if you will excuse the cliché, they are still finger-licking good.

Chicken drummettes or mid-joint wings	1 kg (2 lb 3 oz)
Salt	$^1/_4$ tsp
Corn flour (cornstarch)	2 Tbsp

Sauce

Light soy sauce	2 Tbsp
Sugar	4 tsp
Corn flour (cornstarch)	$1^1/_2$ tsp
Water	4 Tbsp
Garlic	4 cloves, peeled and finely grated
Cooking oil	$^1/_2$ Tbsp

- Wash and drain chicken very well. Mix the chicken with the salt and corn flour. If the flour cakes, a little water, about 1–2 tsp, may be added to help the corn flour coat the chicken better.

- Cover the chicken and chill in the fridge for at least a good 2 hours or overnight.

- Preheat the oven to 240°C (475°F) or 220°C (425°F) for a fan-assisted oven.

- Line a baking tray with aluminium foil and non-stick baking paper.

- Arrange chicken on the tray, spaced slightly apart. Cook for 15 minutes. Turn the chicken wings over and cook for a further 15 minutes.

- While the chicken is in the oven, prepare the sauce. Stir the light soy sauce, sugar, corn flour and water together in a frying pan.

- In another pan big enough to accommodate the chicken, gently sauté the garlic in the oil for a couple of minutes. Use a small flame to avoid browning the garlic. You merely want to cook the garlic to take away its raw pungent flavour.

- Stir the sauce and pour it into the cooked garlic and oil. Increase the flame to medium and stir until the sauce comes to a boil and thickens. Remove from heat.

- When the wings are cooked, remove them from the oven. Transfer the wings to the pan and toss to coat them with the garlic-soy sauce. Serve immediately.

breaded chicken chops with thai salad

serves 4–6

The zesty tastes of Thai food never fail to awaken the senses. The combination of savoury, sweet, tangy, spicy and fragrant flavours tingles, excites and whets the appetite. Breaded chicken chops that are usually fried in oil over the stove can be oven-fried to perfection. Add a refreshing salad drizzled generously with a special Thai sauce and you get a dish in which all of the above flavours come together perfectly.

For the best results, use boneless chicken legs that are about 200 g (7 oz) each. Bigger pieces will yield too much juice during the baking process, resulting in soggy breadcrumbs. The skin should be left on as it contributes the fats to fry the chicken. It also fries to a delicious crisp. The chicken seller will de-bone the legs for you. Keep the bones for making stock. The chicken needs to be thoroughly chilled before baking to prevent it from overcooking given the long cooking time in the oven.

This Thai sauce sings with bright breezy flavours. You can make two portions and freeze one for another time. If you are freezing the sauce, omit the coriander and kaffir lime leaves as they won't retain their colours well in the freezer. Add them when only when the sauce is thawed.

Boneless chicken legs	4, about 200 g (7 oz) each
Salt	1/2 tsp
Corn flour (cornstarch)	2 tsp
Cooking oil	4 Tbsp
Breadcrumbs	250 g (9 oz)

Salad

Cucumber	1 large, peeled
Carrot	1 small, peeled
Red onion	1/2 small, peeled
Red chilli	1, seeded
Coriander leaves (cilantro)	1 stalk

Sauce

Black prawn (shrimp) paste (*hae ko*)	1/2 tsp
Hot water	1 Tbsp
Kaffir lime leaves	2 large
Torch ginger bud	8
Coriander leaves (cilantro)	1 stalk
Sugar	2 tsp
Thai chilli sauce	3 Tbsp
Lime juice	2 Tbsp
Fish sauce	2 Tbsp

- Wash and drain chicken very well. Rub the salt and corn flour all over the chicken and leave them to chill thoroughly in the fridge for at least 2 hours or overnight.

- Prepare the salad. Slice the cucumber in half lengthwise and remove the core. Cut the cucumber and the carrot into long thin strips. Put the strips together on a plate and dry them well with kitchen towels.

- Thinly slice the onion and chilli. Reserve a pretty sprig of coriander leaves for the garnish and cut the rest into roughly 1-cm (1/2-in) lengths. Mix all the vegetables together and chill them in the fridge.

- To prepare the sauce, dissolve the black prawn paste in the hot water. Remove the central veins from the kaffir lime leaves. Thinly slice the leaves and the ginger bud petals. Roughly chop up the coriander leaves, stalks and roots. Mix all the sauce ingredients together. Taste the sauce and adjust seasoning as desired. Leave the sauce in the fridge to chill.

- Preheat the oven to 240°C (475°F) or 220°C (425°F) for a fan-assisted oven.

- Put the oil in a bowl and the breadcrumbs in a plate or casserole dish. Line a baking tray with aluminium foil and non-stick baking paper.

- Take the chicken out of the fridge. Rub each piece with oil and coat generously with breadcrumbs. The oil helps the crumbs adhere to the chicken. Place the chicken skin side down on the prepared tray and bake for 15 minutes. Turn the chicken to the other side and bake for another 10–15 minutes. Chicken should be charmingly golden brown.

- Transfer the chicken immediately to a serving plate. Let them cool a little and cut them up with a pair of kitchen scissors. Drizzle some sauce over. Pile the salad over or serve salad on the side. Serve with the extra sauce in a small dish.

crispy teriyaki chicken chops *serves 4*

These breaded chicken chops are oven-fried in exactly the same way as the breaded chicken chops with Thai salad (page 82). You can use store bought teriyaki sauce or make your own, as I have done here. I used to make an adulterated version, using homemade glutinous rice wine instead of mirin. I had looked up the ingredients for mirin: they are the same as those for making glutinous rice wine, so why not? But understandably you may not have any homemade glutinous rice wine at hand, so the recipe for teriyaki sauce here is made using mirin.

   You can serve these chops as part of a meal, or in bowls of Japanese shortgrain rice, topped with sliced cucumber, shredded lettuce, teriyaki sauce and a generous dollop of Japanese mayonnaise.

Boneless chicken legs	4, about 200 g (7 oz) each
Salt	$^1/_2$ tsp
Corn flour (cornstarch)	2 tsp
Cooking oil	125 ml (4 fl oz / $^1/_2$ cup)
Breadcrumbs	250 g (9 oz)

Teriyaki sauce

Mirin (or homemade glutinous rice wine)	125 ml (4 fl oz / $^1/_2$ cup)
Sake	4 Tbsp
Light soy sauce	4 Tbsp
Sugar	2 Tbsp

- Wash and drain chicken well. Marinate with salt and corn flour. Cover and leave in the fridge to chill for at least 2 hours or overnight.

- To make teriyaki sauce, put all ingredients into a small pot. Bring everything to a boil, and simmer until the sauce reduces by half and thickens enough to coat a spoon—about the consistency of caramel.

- Preheat the oven to 240°C (475°F) or 220°C (425°F) for a fan-assisted oven.

- Line a baking tray with foil and non-stick baking paper. Put breadcrumbs in a plate or casserole dish. Take the chicken out of the fridge. Rub each piece of chicken with oil, then coat with the breadcrumbs. Place the breaded chicken skin side down on the prepared tray.

- Roast in the oven for 15 minutes. Turn the chicken over and roast for another 15 minutes.

- Take the crispy chicken out of the oven and let them cool a little. Slice and arrange on a serving plate. Drizzle teriyaki sauce over. Serve immediately.

thai pandan chicken *serves 4–5*

To make Thai pandan chicken without the hassle of wrapping and deep-frying, the oven is again the appliance of choice. Marinating the chicken in pandan juice will imbue it with the aromatic and pleasing fragrance of this Asian leaf, much more than merely wrapping the chicken with it.

Chicken legs	4, about 250 g (9 oz) each, bone-in
Lemongrass	2 stalks, 5-cm (2-in) from root end, thinly sliced
Garlic	2 cloves, peeled and chopped
Pandan juice (page 13)	1 Tbsp
Coriander powder	1/2 tsp
Ground white pepper	1/2 tsp
Salt	3/4 tsp
Sugar	1 tsp
Fish sauce	1 tsp
Corn flour (cornstarch)	6 Tbsp

- Cut each chicken leg into 4 pieces. Get the chicken seller to do this for you. Wash and drain the chicken legs well.

- Pound lemongrass and garlic into a fine paste.

- Marinate the chicken legs with the entire list of ingredients. Cover with cling film and leave to chill well in the fridge for at least 2 hours or overnight.

- Preheat the oven to 240°C (475°F) or 220°C (425°F) for a fan-assisted oven.

- Line a baking tray with aluminium foil and non-stick baking paper. Arrange the chicken on the tray without overlapping so that each piece of chicken can be adequately exposed to the heat.

- Roast in the oven for 15 minutes. Turn the chicken over and continue to roast for another 15 minutes.

- Transfer the pandan chicken pieces to a serving plate and serve immediately.

lemon chicken *serves 4–5*

This dish will be a hit with children just as sweet and sour pork usually is. I use boneless chicken legs here as with breaded chicken with thai salad. These breaded chicken chops are also oven-fried, then sliced and drizzled with lemon sauce. As an option, cut the chicken into cubes and skewer with slices of cucumber and tomatoes.

Boneless chicken legs	4, about 200 g (7 oz) each
Corn flour (cornstarch)	2 tsp
Salt	1/2 tsp
Cooking oil	4 Tbsp
Breadcrumbs	250 g (9 oz)

Lemon sauce

Lemon juice	4 Tbsp
Water	125 ml (4 fl oz / 1/2 cup)
Salt	1 tsp
Sugar	4 Tbsp
Corn flour (cornstarch)	1 Tbsp
Cooking oil	1 Tbsp
Garlic	2 cloves, peeled and finely grated

- Wash and drain chicken well. Marinate with corn flour, salt and oil. Cover and leave in the fridge to chill for at least 2 hours or overnight.

- Preheat the oven to 240°C (475°F) or 220°C (425°F) for a fan-assisted oven. Line a baking tray with foil and non-stick baking paper. Put breadcrumbs in a plate or casserole dish.
  Take the chicken out of the fridge. Rub each piece of chicken with oil, then coat with the breadcrumbs. Place the breaded chicken skin side down on the prepared tray.

- Bake for 15 minutes. Turn the chicken over and bake for another 15 minutes.

- While the chicken is cooking, mix the lemon juice, water, salt, sugar and corn flour together.

- When the chicken is done, remove the tray from the oven. Heat the oil in a small wok and sauté the garlic over a small flame till lightly golden. Give the lemon sauce a stir and add it all at once to the wok, stirring at the same time. Increase the flame to medium and cook until the sauce boils and thickens. Remove from the heat.

- Slice the chicken. Arrange the slices on a serving plate and drizzle lemon sauce over.

lemongrass chicken with peanut sauce

serves 4–6

My attempts at grilling satay in the oven didn't turn out well. It was a classic case of not doing what I preached. I forgot that smaller thin pieces of meat will not fair well in the oven. They will dry out in the time it takes to brown them. The chicken satay did get cooked (overcooked in fact) and even browned in bits. But the meat lost so much moisture it was hardly a pleasure to eat. The most essential part of satay—that tantalising smoky barbecue flavour that makes satay worth eating was conspicuously absent.

I refused to give up though. Why not cook a whole piece of boneless chicken leg, and then serve it sliced, with onion, cucumber, pineapple chunks and peanut sauce? Definitely doable. Add some cubes of *ketupat* (compressed rice) and a complete meal can be had. This method of cooking negates the time consuming process of skewering small pieces of meat onto sticks. Because you are not eating sticks of satay, you will not be conditioned to expect that smoky flavour. Trust me, you won't miss it either. You might even think this a novel way to eat satay.

The peanut sauce is fairly thick, the way a satay sauce should be. It will coat the chicken and salad vegetables well.

Some satay sauce recipes make use of crunchy peanut butter for a simpler approach. I have decided against that as peanut butter gives the sauce a very soft texture that is not exactly appealing. On the other hand, roasted peanuts, easily ground in a blender, add texture and bite to the sauce.

I usually make a double portion of this sauce (same amount of work) and freeze the extra for a meal of gado-gado, the Indonesian salad of blanched cabbage, long beans, bean sprouts, fried bean curd, sweet crunchy cucumber and *ketupat*. This is the sauce that accompanies gado-gado. Topped with some *keropok* (prawn crackers) and you have another tasty one-dish meal.

This sauce can also be used for another local favourite—satay bee hoon. It is a bit thick for this dish though. You will need to dilute the sauce with some water and adjust the seasoning.

Boneless chicken legs	4, about 200 g (7 oz) each
Lemongrass	4 stalks, 5-cm (2-in) of root end only, sliced
Garlic	2 large cloves, peeled and roughly minced
Turmeric powder	2 tsp
Coriander powder	1 tsp
Salt	1 tsp
Sugar	4 Tbsp
Corn flour (cornstarch)	3 Tbsp
Cooking oil	1 Tbsp

Peanut sauce

Roasted peanuts	180 g (6$^1/_3$ oz)
Tamarind paste	1 Tbsp
Water	250 ml (8 fl oz / 1 cup)
Bottled sambal *belacan*	3 Tbsp
Coriander powder	2 Tbsp
Cumin powder	1 tsp
Coconut milk	250 ml (8 fl oz / 1 cup)
Sugar	3 Tbsp
Salt	to taste

Salad

Onion	1 small, peeled
Cucumber	1 medium
Pineapple	$^1/_2$ small, peeled
Ketupat (optional)	3–4

- Wash and drain chicken chops well. Pound the lemongrass and garlic to a fine paste. Marinate the chicken with the paste and the rest of the ingredients. Cover and chill in the fridge for at least 2 hours or overnight.

- Preheat the oven to 240°C (475°F) or 220°C (425°F) for a fan-assisted oven. Line a baking tray with aluminium foil and non-stick baking paper.

- Arrange the well-chilled chicken skin side down on the tray, spaced apart. Roast for 15 minutes on one side and 10 minutes on the other side. Remove and allow to rest until ready to serve.

- To prepare sauce, grind the peanuts coarsely using the pulse button on your blender. Transfer the peanuts to a bowl.

- Mix tamarind paste with half the water. Strain liquid.

- In a pot, mix the sambal *belacan*, coriander and cumin powders with the remaining water. Drain the tamarind liquid into the pot. Add the coconut milk, sugar and peanuts. Bring everything to a boil and simmer gently for 5 minutes. The sauce will gradually thicken as it simmers. Taste and adjust seasoning as desired.

- To prepare the salad, slice the onion, cucumber and pineapple. Cut the *ketupat* into cubes.

- Assemble the dish by slicing the chicken. Arrange the chicken, onion, cucumber, pineapple and *ketupat* on a big serving plate or on individual plates. Transfer peanut sauce into a big bowl or small individual bowls and serve together.

tandoori chicken *serves 4*

Although tandoori chicken is traditionally cooked in the fiery heat of a tandoor, it is more often than not, deep-fried by the hawkers here. Once again, we will be frying this chicken in the oven.

The tandoori spice paste I use is purchased from an Indian stall at the wet market where there are heaps of ground spice pastes in various shades of terracotta red, yellow ochre and raw sienna. When I ask for tandoori spice paste, the stallholder always gathers a small amount from several of those mounds. No amount of coaxing would make him reveal the proportions and content of the spice paste, but he would always advise me against artificially colouring the tandoori chicken the customary red as he insists that authentic tandoori chicken is not red at all.

If you use a commercially prepared tandoori paste purchased from a supermarket, follow the package instruction on the proportion of paste to chicken.

Chicken legs	4, about 200 g (7 oz) each, with skin on
Tandoori spice paste	6 Tbsp
Cooking oil	1 Tbsp
Salt	1 tsp

- Wash and drain chicken well. Separate the thighs from the drumsticks to get 8 pieces of chicken.

- Stir the tandoori spice paste, oil and salt well to combine the different spices properly.

- Smear the paste on the chicken flesh under as well as on the skin. Cover and chill in the fridge for 2 hours or overnight.

- Preheat the oven to 240°C (475°F) or 220°C (425°F) for a fan-assisted oven. Line a 30 x 20-cm (11 x 7-in) baking tray with non-stick baking paper.

- Place chicken skin side down on the prepared tray, spacing them out slightly. Roast for 15 minutes. Turn the chicken pieces over and continue to roast for another 15 minutes.

- Remove the tray from the oven. Let the chicken rest for about 10 minutes before serving.

samosa rolls *makes about 25 rolls*

These cigar-size samosa rolls just seem much more fun to eat than the traditional triangular ones, which makes them perfect finger food. That they can be made in advance and baked just prior to being served is an added point in their favour. Arrange the prepared samosa rolls on trays and store in the fridge. Serve immediately after baking—the crispy exterior will crumble into shards as you take a bite.

Potatoes	3 medium, about 200 g (7 oz) each
Cooking oil	1 Tbsp
Onion	1 medium, peeled and diced
Garlic	2 cloves, peeled and finely minced
Curry powder	1 Tbsp
Bottled sambal *belacan*	1 Tbsp
Chicken broth or water	125–250 ml (4–8 fl oz / $^1/_2$–1 cup)
Peas	65 g ($2^1/_3$ oz)
Salt	$1^1/_4$ tsp
Sugar	1 tsp
Spring roll skin	about 50 pieces, 12 x 12-cm (5 x 5-in) each
Cooking oil	125 ml (4 fl oz / $^1/_2$ cup)

- Scrub the potatoes well and put them in a pot. Fill with enough water to submerge the potatoes. Bring to a boil and simmer until potatoes are cooked through, about 30 minutes.

- When the potatoes are cooked, drain and peel them. Cut the potatoes into 1-cm ($^1/_2$-in) cubes.

- Heat the oil in a non-stick wok. Fry the onion over a gentle heat until softened and on the verge of browning. Toss in the garlic and sauté until both garlic and onion start to brown. Add the curry powder and sambal *belacan* at this point, stirring until everything is well combined.

- Add the potatoes, 125 ml (4 fl oz / $^1/_2$ cup) chicken broth or water, peas, salt and sugar. Cook together, mixing well. Let the filling simmer for a little bit, allowing the potatoes to absorb some of the fragrant spices. Add more water and let the potatoes cook until they clump together. You may not need all the remaining water. When the liquid has been absorbed, turn off the flame. Check and adjust seasoning. Allow filling to cool.

- Get ready the spring roll skin, oil, a pastry brush and two 30 x 20-cm (11 x 7-in) baking trays lined with non-stick baking paper.

- Use a clean chopping board to make the rolls. Lay a piece of skin on the board. Brush evenly with oil as well. Place another piece of skin on top, brushing that with oil. Spread about 1 rounded Tbsp filling along the edge of the skin nearest to you. Push the filling into a sausage shape, leaving about 1-cm ($^1/_2$-in) between the filling and the edge of the skin at both ends. This is to ensure that the filling does not ooze out when you roll. Roll up the samosa all the way. Put the finished rolls on the tray, making sure they are spaced slightly apart. Continue until all the filling is used up.

- Preheat the oven to 220°C (425°F). Bake or "fry", if you will, these rolls for 25–30 minutes until golden brown. Serve immediately.

roast

Roasting is a dry-heat cooking method. Traditionally it is done on a spit over an open fire. The meat can be a whole animal or a large cut like a leg of lamb. Since most of us live in high-rise flats without any access to wide open spaces, we are unable to do any such roasting. But thankfully we can move this entire operation into the oven.

Most ovens come fitted with a rotisserie and a drip pan made of heavy-duty metal to catch the fat and meat juices that drip off the meat as it roasts. I prefer roasting the meat on a tray or the drip pan itself—the less fuss the better.

Whole poultry, a rack of prime ribs, smaller pieces of pork ribs, pork belly and whole strips of pork or beef fillet can be roasted in the oven. The time required will differ according to the size, weight, thickness and temperature of the meat.

Basting is not necessary as it does not add to the moisture of the roast. The fat content of the meat, the kind of marinade (moist or dry), the oven temperature and especially the length of cooking time, are factors that determine the moisture level of the roasted product. When meat cooks, it will exude juices and shrink. The longer it cooks, the more juices will be lost. The trick then is to roast at the optimum temperature for the particular weight of the meat, and for the right length of time to minimise moisture loss.

Besides meat, vegetables like aubergines and onions, and tubers like carrots and potatoes also take well to roasting. Leafy vegetables are a no-no. The leaves will just dry up and take on the texture of paper—an extremely unappetising prospect.

Roasting may seem like a complex cooking method that is difficult to master but it is, in actual fact, quite simple. Practise and acquire a working knowledge of how your oven handles roasting. If your initial attempt comes up short, all is not lost. Even a burnt roast can be salvaged to make a tasty stock by removing all the burnt bits first. In any event, if you read through these recipes properly and follow the instructions carefully, you will reap the flavoursome rewards of your labour.

roasting chicken

It is my belief that if you do not learn to cook anything else, you must at least pick up the skill to roast a chicken. A whole roast chicken on a platter looks so elegant, delectable and enticing. Yet there is nothing mind-boggling about its preparation. Just learn a few technicalities of roasting and you are on your way.

Firstly, choose a smaller chicken for the best skin to meat ratio. This proportion is crucial to the flavour we are going to coax out of the chicken; it is really why we love our chicken wings, isn't it? The marinade is not going to penetrate deep into the thick flesh of a big fat bird, the reason why I have never understood the appeal of turkey. Why do you think the Christmas turkey is always served with some sort of gravy? Isn't it to mask the fact that the flesh is tasteless? So go with a chicken weighing roughly between 1 and 1.2 kg (2 lb 3 oz and 2 lb 6 oz). Roast two if you're feeding a crowd.

Secondly, for the meat to be infused with the flavours of the marinade, it just makes sense to marinate it as well as the skin. Hence for all the roast chicken recipes in this book, you'll have to separate the skin from the meat and insert most of the marinade ingredients under the skin. This is probably the only part of the whole process that requires just a bit more elbow grease. But it is well worth the effort.

Thirdly, the chicken must be at room temperature when you put it into the oven. This will make certain that the whole chicken is cooked through at the end of the specified cooking time. If you marinate the chicken a day before, which is what I always do, then you have to take it out of the fridge a few hours before roasting it.

Finally, when it comes to the actual roasting,

I tend to ignore the rotisserie. It is simply too bothersome. I prefer to use a roasting tray lined with two layers of aluminium foil and a piece of non-stick baking paper. You don't want to remove the chicken from the tray only to have the skin stuck to it. So the non-stick paper is essential.

Once the chicken is roasted, take the whole tray out of the oven. Let the chicken rest in the tray for 20–30 minutes before cutting. This allows the chicken to reabsorb the juices and be really succulent when you eat it. In one of my first few attempts at roasting a chicken, I was too anxious to wait and cut the chicken up almost immediately once it came out of the oven. Just one cut and the juices flowed out. This is why I never insert a knife into the thickest part of the thigh to check if the chicken is cooked, as proposed in many cookbooks. A small chicken at room temperature will be nicely roasted in about 30 minutes in a very hot oven while two will take about 40 minutes.

If you are using a counter top oven in which the heating elements are considerably closer to the chicken, you'll find that the chicken may be quite adequately browned about 20 minutes into the cooking time. Just cover the chicken loosely with foil to prevent the skin from being burnt and continue roasting for the remaining time.

That's about it. Now we're all set... let's make some roast chickens.

simple roast chicken *serves 4–6*

This is a basic roast chicken, using a minimum of marinade ingredients but absolutely not short on taste. The salt may seem excessive but it really brings out the full flavour of the chicken. A bland roast chicken is simply not worth eating.

Chicken	1, about 1 kg (2 lb 3 oz)
Salt	1^1/$_2$ tsp
Ground white pepper	1^1/$_2$ tsp
Light soy sauce	1^1/$_2$ tsp
Coriander leaves (cilantro)	1 large stalk, cut into 1-cm (^{1}/$_2$-in) lengths

- Wash the chicken and dry it well with kitchen towels.

- Mix the salt and pepper together in a small dish.

- Using your fingers, gently separate the skin from the meat, starting from one side of the chicken breast. Be careful not to poke any holes in the skin. Work all the way to the thigh and the end of the drumstick. Now do the same to the other half of the chicken.

- Rub light soy sauce all over the chicken skin. Use a ^{1}/$_4$-tsp measuring spoon and scoop some of the salt-pepper mixture. Start with one side of the chicken first. Insert the spoon under the skin all the way to the drumstick area. Turn the spoon over to deposit the contents there. Scoop more of the marinade mixture and drop this on the thigh under the skin. Next pick up some more marinade and deposit this on the chicken breast under the skin. Insert your fingers under the skin and rub the marinade evenly over the drumstick, thigh and chicken breast.

- Repeat this process on the other half of the chicken. Rub the remaining marinade on the wings and the skin of the chicken. Tuck the wing tips behind. Leave to marinate for 2 hours or overnight.

- Line a roasting tray with foil and non-stick baking paper. Preheat the oven to 240°C (475°F) or 220°C (425°F) for a fan-assisted oven. When the oven is ready, put the chicken on the tray breast side up and roast for 30 minutes.

- Take the chicken out of the oven and leave it to rest for 20–30 minutes.

- There will be some juices in the chicken cavity. Pour this out into a cup or bowl. Pour the juices (there shouldn't be much when the chicken is cooked just right) and the oil from the roasting tray into the same cup or bowl. Cut the chicken. A pair of kitchen scissors does this well. Arrange the pieces on a serving plate. Skim off the oil from the meat juices and drizzle the latter over the chicken. Top with coriander leaves.

black pepper roast chicken *serves 4–6*

I am not sure if black pepper roast chicken can be categorised as Asian. They are not found in the menus of western restaurants or cookbooks though a good many of these can be seen at the roast meat counters of the major supermarkets here. Most likely they are a local creation. I suppose sales of these chickens are brisk or they would disappear from the scene soon enough. Heck, I've bought one myself and was disappointed that there was not much in the way of a deep black peppery flavour. This only prompted me to try roasting one.

Black pepper shares a surprisingly apt affinity with dark soy sauce, so that seemed a promising place to start. It should be black peppercorns that you have dry-fried and coarsely ground. Chew these rugged bits and the intense peppery fragrance will burst forth in the mouth. The next ingredient would be salt; roast chickens of any kind crave salt. Just these three simple ingredients for the marinade—can't be any easier. My son has declared this to be the tastiest roast chicken he has ever eaten. But then he says that about every kind of roast chicken that comes out of the oven.

This chicken looks scarily blackish as a result of the dark soy sauce. But it is not burnt at all.

Chicken	1, about 1 kg (2 lb 3 oz)
Salt	$1^1/_2$ tsp
Coarsely ground black pepper	$1^1/_2$ Tbsp
Superior dark soy sauce	2 tsp

- Wash the chicken and dry it well with kitchen towels.

- Mix the salt and ground black pepper together in a small dish. Get a $^1/_4$-tsp measuring spoon ready.

- Using your fingers, gently separate the skin from the meat, starting from one side of the chicken breast. Be careful not to poke any holes in the skin. Work all the way to the thigh and the end of the drumstick. Now do the same to the other half of the chicken.

- Beginning with one side of the chicken, rub $^1/_2$ tsp dark soy sauce on the meat under the skin on the breast, the thigh and the drumstick. Do the same to the other half of the chicken.

- Using the same method as the previous roast chicken recipe (page 100), deposit and rub the salt and pepper mixture under the skin. Finally rub the remaining salt and dark soy sauce on the skin. Tuck the wings tips behind.

- Leave to marinate for at least 2 hours or overnight.

- Preheat the oven to 240°C (475°F) or 220°C (425°F) for a fan-assisted oven.

- Line a roasting tin with foil and non-stick baking paper. Place the chicken in the tin. Roast for 30 minutes.

- Remove the chicken from the oven and let it rest for 20–30 minutes before cutting and serving.

roast pork *serves 8–10*

The roast pork sold at hawker centres and food courts in Singapore tend to be a little tough for my taste. I prefer roast pork to be tender, the fats meltingly soft and the skin crispy. I only eat the sides that have been caramelised during the roasting. They are also the most flavourful parts where the marinade resides.

To make your own roast pork, you need to get the pork in one square or rectangular piece. Thin strips of pork belly are not suitable as these have more surface area exposed to the heat, causing the meat to lose considerable moisture during the time needed to roast and crisp the skin.

I employ a long, slow cooking time at a low temperature so the pork can retain most of its juices yet allow the fats to cook to a tender jelly and the skin to slowly dry out. The last 10 minutes or so of cooking time will be at a high temperature to crisp the skin.

The piece of pork belly does not come with uniform thickness, thus you will need two metal skewers that must be inserted diagonally, as near to the skin as possible to maintain a level surface for the skin to crisp more evenly. As the pork cooks in the oven it will expand in height. Without the metal skewers, the surface will undulate during the expansion, making it impossible to obtain the consistent brown and crispy skin we are after. Because our ovens are slightly different, and the distance from the skin to the grill being another variable, you will have to be watchful during the skin crisping part to ensure that the skin does not burn. There may be bits of burnt parts here and there due to the slight unevenness of the skin and the unequal distribution of heat in the oven. These can be scraped off later.

It is very important that the roast pork is adequately rested for 20–30 minutes so it can re-absorb the meat juices. Slice with a very sharp knife that can cut through the crispy skin neatly.

Pork belly	1, about 1 kg (2 lb 3 oz)
Salt	2 tsp
Coarsely ground black pepper	1 tsp
Five-spice powder (optional)	a pinch
Cucumber slices	to garnish

- Wash the pork belly and dry it well with kitchen towels. Remove any remnant hair on the skin with a pair of tweezers.

- Score the skin at 1-cm ($^1/_2$-in) intervals using a very sharp knife. Be careful not to cut into the lean meat below. Make another set of cuts diagonal to the first set. The scoring increases the surface area of the skin that is exposed to the heat, helping to create a crispy crackling.

- Leave the meat in the fridge to dry for a few hours or overnight but you must let the pork come to room temperature before roasting.

- Take the pork out of the fridge. Dry it again with kitchen towels. Rub $^1/_2$ tsp salt on the skin. Rub the black pepper, the remaining salt and the five-spice powder (if using) on the rest of the meat. Leave to marinate till the meat is at room temperature.

- Preheat the oven to 150°C (300°F). Line a baking tray with foil and non-stick baking paper.

- Starting from one corner of the pork, insert a metal skewer just under the skin, threading it diagonally all the way to the opposite corner. Do the same with another skewer, this time starting from another corner. The two skewers should form an X.

- Put the pork on the tray skin side up and bake in the oven for 1 hour 30 minutes. Now turn on the grill function. Grill the skin for 5–10 minutes, checking frequently. The skin should blister and crisp all over.

- Take the pork out of the oven. Let the pork rest for at least 20–30 minutes before removing the skewers. Scrape off any burnt bits of skin. Cut the roast pork into bite-size pieces and serve with slices of cucumber.

barbecued pork char siew *serves 4–5*

Garishly orange or red barbecued pork (*char siew*) is a huge turn off. Is the bright colour meant to contrast with the white centre of the sliced meat and hence make the *char siew* more appealing? I prefer barbecued pork that takes on the deep dark brown of the marinade, is burnt in parts, and without any unnaturally fabricated colour scheme.

Making your own barbecued pork is easier than you would expect. The marinade ingredients are things you would have in your kitchen as a matter of course. Many barbecued pork recipes require maltose, a thick honey-like syrup that comes in a tub. It is used in Peking duck, mooncakes and Chinese barbecued pork ribs. Unless you cook any of these, or intend to, with regularity, your tub of maltose would simply be a squatter in a piece of prime real estate that is your kitchen. For practical reasons, honey is a good substitute, or more conveniently, simply use sugar, as I have done here.

Shoulder butt, a relatively cheap cut of meat, is used for making barbecued pork. It comes in a thick oval shaped slice, rather like a huge steak. It is marbled with fat, making it ideal for grilling or roasting. Incidentally, this cut is not from the rear end of the pig, but from the shoulder. In eighteenth century America, "butts" was another name for the barrels in which these meats were stored and shipped.

If you purchase the shoulder butt from the wet market, the butcher will help you cut the slice of pork into a long strip. You can do this yourself if you buy the meat from the supermarket. Place the meat flat on the chopping board. Imagine two horizontal perforated lines on the meat, dividing it into thirds. Starting from the right edge, cut along one of these imaginary lines, but stop about 2-cm (1-in) from the left edge. Now start from the left edge—cut along the other line and stop about 2-cm (1-in) from the right. Finally, pull the meat gently into a long strip.

You can roast several strips of barbecued pork simultaneously, as long as your baking tray can accommodate. But they must be placed with some space between them to allow for proper heat circulation to aid the browning.

Ginger	1 thumb-size knob, peeled and finely grated
Garlic	4 cloves, peeled and finely grated
Dark soy sauce	1$\frac{1}{2}$ Tbsp
Water	4 Tbsp
Sugar	6 Tbsp
Salt	1$\frac{1}{2}$ tsp
Corn flour (cornstarch)	1 tsp
Cooking oil	1 Tbsp
Pork shoulder butt	2 strips, about 300 g (10$\frac{1}{2}$ oz) each

- Mix all the ingredients except pork together.
- Put the pork into the marinade, coating it well. Cover and chill in the fridge for 1 hour or more. For this recipe, the pork must be cold when it goes into the oven.
- Preheat the oven to 240°C (475°F) or 220°C (425°F) for a fan-assisted oven.
- Line a baking tray with foil and non-stick baking paper.
- When the oven is ready, take the meat out from the fridge. Arrange the meat on the tray. Be sure to space the strips of meat apart for better heat circulation. Roast for 15 minutes on one side. Turn the meat over and roast for another 10–15 minutes.
- Take the roasted meat out of the oven. Let the meat rest for about 15 minutes before slicing.
- In the meantime, heat the remaining marinade in a small pot, stirring frequently till the sauce bubbles.
- Slice the meat. Arrange on a plate and drizzle with the sauce. Serve this with cucumber slices and sprigs of coriander leaves.

vietnamese lemongrass pork *serves 4–6*

This is very similar to barbecued pork (page 106), as it uses the same method and same cut of pork with only a few differences in the ingredients used. Instead of salt, fish sauce—one of the essential ingredients in Vietnamese cuisine—imparts an interesting salinity to the meat here. This lemongrass pork is not quite as sweet as barbecued pork, hence the reduced amount of sugar. But this is a variable you can tweak to suit your own taste.

Serve this pork with rice or a vermicelli salad.

Lemongrass	3 stalks, 5-cm (2-in) of root end only
Garlic	3 cloves, peeled and finely grated
Sugar	3 Tbsp
Fish sauce	2 Tbsp
Cooking oil	1 Tbsp
Corn flour (cornstarch)	1 Tbsp
Pork shoulder butt	2 strips, about 300 g (10$\frac{1}{2}$ oz) each

- Slice the lemongrass thinly, then pound or chop it coarsely. The rough grilled bits of lemongrass are fun to chew.

- Combine all the ingredients except pork in a bowl. Coat the pork well with the marinade. Cover and chill in the fridge for 1–2 hours. The pork must be well chilled when it goes into the oven.

- Preheat the oven to 240°C (475°F) or 220°C (425°F) for a fan-assisted oven. Line a tray with foil and non-stick baking paper.

- When the oven has reached the desired temperature, take the pork out of the fridge and arrange on the tray. Baste with some of the leftover marinade. Roast for 15 minutes. Turn the pork over and baste with the remaining marinade. Roast for another 15 minutes.

- Take the pork out of the oven. Rest the pork for 15 minutes before slicing to serve.

vietnamese meatballs *makes 12 large meatballs*

These meatballs are a variation of the Vietnamese meatloaf. They cook in a short time at a high temperature that enhances caramelisation. The meat mixture must be well chilled to prevent overcooking while the exterior browns. These meatballs are soft when hot, but will set to a firmer texture when cooled. Whichever way you like them, serve with *nuoc cham*, that pungent, briny, tangy and spicy dipping sauce that for me is an indispensable part of a Vietnamese meal.

Meatballs

Minced pork	300 g (10^1/$_2$ oz)
Water	4^1/$_2$ Tbsp
Black fungus	1, soaked and chopped
Fried vermicelli	20 g (^{2}/$_3$ oz), soaked to soften and cut into 1-cm (^{1}/$_2$-in) lengths
Spring onions (scallion)	2, diced
Garlic	1 large clove, peeled and finely grated
Carrot	^{1}/$_3$, peeled and grated
Sandwich bread	1^1/$_2$ slices, finely diced
Egg	1
Fish sauce	1 Tbsp
Ground white pepper	^{1}/$_2$ tsp
Cooking oil	as needed

Dipping sauce

Red bird's eye chilli	2, seeded and chopped
Garlic	2 cloves, peeled and finely grated
Fish sauce	1 Tbsp
Water	1 Tbsp
Vinegar	1 Tbsp
Sugar	1 tsp

- Mix pork with water. Combine all ingredients for meatballs, except oil, in a mixing bowl. Cover with cling film and chill in the fridge for at least 2 hours.

- To cook the meatballs, preheat the oven to 220°C (425°F).

- Line a 30 x 20-cm (11 x 7-in) baking tray with non-stick baking paper. Divide the meat mixture into 12 portions. Shape each into a ball and coat thinly with oil. Arrange on the tray, spaced slightly apart. Bake for 20 minutes.

- Meanwhile, combine sauce ingredients in a dipping bowl, stirring until the sugar dissolves. Adjust seasoning to taste.

- Transfer meatballs to a serving plate and serve with the dipping sauce on the side.

black pepper ribs *serves 4–6*

When roasting ribs in the oven, wet marinades work better to give a moist layer of caramelised glaze on the meat. Dry marinades are doable too, but the marinated meats have to be coated with a layer of oil to keep it moist.

When eating ribs, the degree of tenderness is a matter of individual taste. I like ribs tender as reflected in the recipe here. Both prime ribs and the more economical spare ribs can be used.

Spare ribs or prime ribs	1 kg (2 lb 3 oz), washed and drained
Water	250 ml (8 fl oz / 1 cup)
Corn flour (cornstarch)	2 Tbsp
Oyster sauce	1 Tbsp
Dark soy sauce	1 tsp
Sugar	1 Tbsp
Salt	1 tsp
Cooking oil	1 Tbsp
Onion	1 medium, peeled and finely diced
Garlic	2 cloves, peeled and minced
Coarsely ground black pepper	1 Tbsp

- Line a baking tray with foil and non-stick baking paper. Arrange the ribs in a single layer on the tray. Cover tightly with foil and cook in the oven at 180°C (350°F) for 1 hour. The oven does not need preheating.

- Stir water, corn flour, oyster sauce, dark soy sauce, sugar and salt in a bowl. Set aside.

- Heat oil in a small pot. Sauté onion over low heat until it starts to brown. Add garlic and black pepper. Continue frying until both onion and garlic brown. Give the liquid ingredients a final stir and add to the onion and garlic. Let everything come to a boil, stirring frequently. The black pepper marinade is done.

- When the ribs have cooked for 1 hour, remove the tray from the oven. Discard foil cover. With a pair of chopsticks, transfer the ribs to a plate. Pour the meat juices in the tray into a cup. You can skim off the fats and freeze the meat juices to make stock or gravy for other dishes.

- Increase the oven temperature to 240°C (475°F) or 220°C (425°F) for a fan-assisted oven.

- Instead of brushing each piece with the marinade, I find it infinitely easier to pick up each piece of rib with chopsticks, dip it in the marinade and place it back on the same tray. Spread any remaining marinade on the ribs.

- Return the ribs to the oven and roast for 6–8 minutes. Turn the ribs over and roast for another 6–8 minutes.

- Transfer the ribs to a serving plate. Scrape any of the caramelised marinade (this is the best bit) from the tray and smear on the ribs. Let the ribs rest for about 10 minutes before serving.

roasted stingray with curry leaves

serves 4

Although I have mentioned that seafood is not a suitable for roasting in the oven, the stingray is an exception as it is the most forgiving of seafood to cook. The stingray is grilled cold from the fridge. This allows it to be in the oven long enough for the exterior to brown while the interior remains moist. The gelatinous texture of the flesh helps it to stay moist and even enables the stingray to take some overcooking without being completely dried out—not that you want to cook it longer than necessary.

I have tried using the grill function for this dish, but found that it actually took longer as the fish was cooked only on one side. The fish then had to be turned for the other side to be cooked. Using the default oven setting with the heat coming from both the top and bottom of the oven and a high temperature, the fish will be roasted on both sides simultaneously, without the need to turn it at all. And it actually browns better.

Stingray fillets	2, 250 g (9 oz) each, cut in half horizontally
Dark soy sauce	1 tsp
Coarsely ground black pepper	1 Tbsp
Salt	1/2 tsp
Oyster sauce	1 tsp
Cooking oil	1 Tbsp
Corn flour (cornstarch)	2 Tbsp
Curry leaves	10 stalks

- Marinate the stingray fillets with all the ingredients. There is no need to remove the curry leaves from the stalks. This way it will be easier to remove the leaves later on. Simply bruise the leaves with a pestle to release the flavour. Leave the stingray in the fridge for at least 2 hours so it gets really cold.

- Preheat the oven to 240°C (475°F) or 220°C (425°F) for a fan-assisted oven. Line a baking tray with foil and non-stick baking paper.

- Remove the sprigs of curry leaves. Lay the fillets skin side down on the tray, well spaced apart.

- Grill the fillets for 10–12 minutes. There is no need to turn them over. Garnish with coriander leaves if desired and serve immediately.

roasted aubergines *serves 4*

This is one of my favourite vegetable dishes from the Malay rice stall. The aubergine is deep-fried whole until the inside is soft and creamy, and then topped with a fragrant fried chilli paste. In this recipe, the aubergine is roasted in the oven, leaving only the chilli paste to be cooked on the stovetop.

Red chillies	8, seeded
Shallots	4, peeled
Garlic	2 cloves, peeled
Dried prawn (shrimp) paste (*belacan*)	1 tsp
Cooking oil	2 Tbsp + more as needed
Water	4 Tbsp
Sugar	1 tsp
Salt	1/2 tsp
Aubergines (eggplants/ brinjals)	2, about 200 g (7 oz) each

- Blend chillies, shallots, garlic, and dried prawn paste with 2 Tbsp oil. Add a bit of water (if needed) to help the blades move.

- Heat a non-stick pot or wok and fry the blended paste over a low flame. There is no need to add oil to the pot or wok, as there is oil in the paste. Fry until the oil separates and the paste is very fragrant.

- Add the water and let the paste simmer for a little while. Stir in the sugar and salt. Taste and adjust seasoning as needed. The chilli paste can be prepared ahead. It freezes very well too.

- To roast aubergines, preheat the oven to 240°C (475°F) or 220°C (425°F) for a fan-assisted oven. Brush aubergines generously with oil and place them on a tray lined with non-stick baking paper. Roast for 20 minutes. Thicker aubergines may require a few more minutes.

- Cut each roasted aubergine into thick slices and arrange the pieces on a plate. Top with the chilli paste.

bake

In Asia, the baking of sweet confectionary is the function most frequently associated with the oven. And if you are as fond of sweet treats as I am, you would get an oven just to bake all these goodies. But there is a wide range of savoury bakes too. Of course in the context of this book, I have added an Asian twist to both categories of bakes—aromatic Asian ingredients are used in all the recipes.

Baking is more of a science than the other cooking methods. The right proportion of dry ingredients (flour and sugar) to the wet ones (butter, eggs, milk or juice) is instrumental to the consistency of a batter or dough. There is only a very small window for manipulation and error. So when baking something for the first time, you need to follow the quantities of ingredients closely, even if you are an instinctive cook. Bend the rules only after you have learnt them and know exactly what you are doing.

For a start, you should refer to the instruction manual of your oven for the correct rack position for the various bakes. I used to have a counter top oven that called for cakes to be baked at the second lowest rack position, contrary to the general rule of baking cakes and cookies in the centre of the oven. When I tried the conventional rack position in that particular oven, the cake came out with a slightly burnt top crust. So knowing your oven is crucial to how successfully you can use it. This bears repeating—the only way to know your oven is to use it.

When baking cookies, the lighter-coloured aluminium trays are preferable. The darker-coloured ones conduct heat more speedily; hence your cookies will have much browner bottoms than the tops.

As I have mentioned earlier, the baking times in this book are estimates and may vary between different ovens to the tune of some 5–10 minutes. Always check the colour and texture of your baked products. Test muffins and cakes by inserting a metal skewer or satay stick into the centres. The skewer should come out clean. Run your fingers along the part of the skewer that was inserted into the cake or muffin. If it feels sticky, or if you see unbaked batter stuck to it, then bake for a further few minutes. Test again to ensure that the cake or muffins are baked before removing from the oven.

I used to be baffled by the calibrations of oven temperatures and cooking times—how did those bakers and cookbook writers know how long and at what temperature to bake anything? I have since found that this knowledge comes with experience. Bake often enough and you will be pleasantly surprised at how you can estimate cooking temperatures and time fairly accurately. As for the occasional mistakes, they are best seen as opportunities to learn.

curry chicken and potato pie *serves 8–12*

The idea of baking a curry chicken and potato pie as opposed to making a pile of curry puffs was born out of laziness. As much as I love fried food, deep-frying is my least favoured method of cooking.

The thought of rolling and re-rolling dough for curry puffs, shaping them one by one, then frying them batch by batch in a pot of oil is not particularly appealing.

A pie though requires only two pieces of dough—for the bottom and top crusts. The baking tin is lined, the filling packed in and then covered with another piece of dough. I am even inspired to decorate the pie creatively with the excess dough. In fact the baking cannot be included as a "step"—the oven is doing the work. All these are perfectly doable, not to mention that a plate of curry puffs does not command the elegance that a beautifully baked golden brown pie does.

Filling

Chicken breast	1
Chicken leg	1
Potatoes	4, about 100 g (3^1/$_2$ oz) each
Cooking oil	1^1/$_2$ Tbsp
Onions	2 medium, peeled and finely diced
Garlic	4 cloves, peeled and finely minced
Water	125–250 ml (4–8 fl oz / ^{1}/$_2$–1 cup)
Bottled sambal *belacan*	1^1/$_2$ Tbsp
Meat or chicken curry powder	2 Tbsp
Salt	1 tsp
Hard-boiled eggs	2, peeled and cut into wedges

Crust

Egg	1, cold from the fridge
Iced water	2–3 Tbsp, with 2 cubes of ice
Plain (all-purpose) flour	250 g (9 oz), cold from the fridge
Salt	^{1}/$_2$ tsp
Unsalted butter	125 g (4^1/$_2$ oz), cold from the fridge and finely diced

• Prepare the filling first. Put the chicken breast and thigh in a small baking tin or tray. Cover tightly with foil and cook in the oven at 200°C (400°F) for 20 minutes. There is no need to preheat the oven. Turn off the oven and leave the chicken inside for another 10 minutes. It will continue to cook in the residual heat. Take the chicken out to cool sufficiently before de-boning and cutting into 1-cm (^{1}/$_2$-in) cubes. Retain the chicken juices.

• Cook the potatoes in boiling water. Peel and cut the potatoes into 1-cm (^{1}/$_2$-in) cubes.

• Heat oil in a non-stick wok. Sauté onions until they begin to brown. Add the garlic. Continue to fry until garlic turns golden brown. Add sambal *belacan* and curry powder.

• Now include the potatoes. Stir to coat everything with the fragrant curry paste. Add 125 ml (4 fl oz / ^{1}/$_2$ cup) water and salt. Stir again and cook for 1–2 minutes until the water is absorbed.

- Add the chicken, its juices and more of the remaining water. Cook until the water is absorbed and the potatoes clump together so the filling will not fall apart when the pie is sliced. Let the filling cool completely.

- To make the crust, break the egg into a bowl. Beat it well and set aside 1 Tbsp (for glazing the pie) in another bowl. Get the iced water with the ice cubes ready. Lay 2 sheets of cling film on the table.

- Mix the flour and salt together in a mixing bowl. Rub the cold dices of butter into the flour until a crumbly mixture is obtained. Add the egg and 2 Tbsp iced water. Mix the liquid ingredients into the flour with your fingers, using a light touch. All the ingredients should come together to form a malleable, non-sticky dough. Add a bit more of the iced water (1 tsp at a time) if the dough is too dry.

- Form two-thirds of the dough into a disc and the remaining one-third into a smaller disc. Wrap each piece of dough with cling film and refrigerate for about 30 minutes.

- Line the bottom of a 22-cm ($8^1/_2$-in) round springform tin with non-stick baking paper. Take out the pieces of dough. I prefer to have the dough protected between 2 pieces of cling film as I roll it. This way, there is no need to dust the dough, tabletop and rolling pin with excess flour to prevent sticking. The excess flour will also alter the butter to flour ratio of the dough resulting in a less buttery pastry. Just make sure that the cling film is big enough to accommodate the dough as you roll. You may need to add an extra piece to avoid rolling the dough onto the tabletop.

- Unwrap the larger piece of dough. Cover the dough with another piece of cling film and roll it out to a circle about 35-cm ($13^1/_2$-in) in diameter. Remove the top piece of cling film. Slide your hand beneath the bottom piece of film and lift the dough up carefully. Gently invert the dough into the springform tin. Ease the dough into the tin and line the bottom and sides of the tin. Trim off the excess overhanging dough. It can be used to patch up any shortfall on the sides. Once the dough is in place, remove the cling film.

- Fill the pie with half the chicken and potato filling. Press down gently to pack the filling tightly. Arrange the egg wedges in a circle on the filling. Add the remaining filling and press down gently again. Level the top.

- Preheat the oven to 220°C (425°F).

- Roll out the smaller piece of dough between 2 sheets of cling film to a circle of 24-cm ($9^1/_2$-in) in diameter. Transfer it to the pie and invert it on top. Remove the cling film. Press the edges of the two pieces of dough together. Trim off the excess with a knife. Use the excess dough to decorate the pie. Brush the top well with the beaten egg that was set aside. Cut some small holes in the top crust. This is to allow steam to escape during baking.

- Bake in the oven for 50 minutes.

- Cool the pie on a rack for at least 30 minutes before unmoulding. The crust becomes crispier and firmer as the pie cools. You can serve this pie warm or at room temperature.

chicken rendang pie *serves 4–6*

This dish was a result of leftover mashed potatoes and *rendang* spice paste sharing space in the freezer. There was no time to prepare beef *rendang*—some 2 hours are needed for the beef to be tender. But chicken *rendang* can cook in half that time.

This seemingly odd pairing turned out unexpectedly good—the creamy mashed potatoes complemented the spice-laden chicken surprisingly well.

Now this *rendang* pie has become a handy potluck dish, as well as a one-dish meal as it is very easy to cook. Best of all, it can be prepared in advance, in a big family-size dish or in smaller single serving portions. I use bone-in chicken parts for this dish (they are juicier), and de-bone the chicken after cooking. To make things even easier, I don't fry the spice mix. This way I minimise the oil content in the *rendang* to make way for the substantial amount of butter I add to the mashed potatoes.

Chicken rendang

Desiccated coconut	40 g (1½ oz)
Onion	1 medium, peeled and roughly chopped
Garlic	2 cloves, peeled and roughly chopped
Lemongrass	1 stalk, 5-cm (2-in) from the root end, thinly sliced
Water	125 ml (4 fl oz / ½ cup)
Coconut powder	1 packet, about 50 g (1⅔ oz)
Meat curry powder	2 Tbsp
Chilli powder	1 Tbsp
Salt	1 tsp
Sugar	2 Tbsp
Chicken legs	4, about 200 g (7 oz) each, thighs and drumsticks separated and skinned
Turmeric leaf	1
Pandan leaves	2
Kaffir lime leaves	8

Mashed potato

Russet potatoes	3, about 200 g (7 oz) each
Milk	125 ml (4 fl oz / ½ cup)
Butter	60 g (2 oz)
Salt	1–1¼ tsp
Ground black pepper	½ tsp
Grated Cheddar or Parmesan	100 g (3½ oz)

- Fry the desiccated coconut over a low flame. Be watchful and stir frequently as the coconut will burn easily. When it starts to turn brown, turn off the flame but continue to toss the coconut as it will brown in the residual heat. Set the coconut aside to cool.

- Grind onion, garlic and lemongrass in a blender together with water. Add 1 Tbsp more water if needed to get the blender going.

- Transfer the ground ingredients into a bowl. Mix in the coconut powder, meat curry powder, chilli powder, salt and sugar.

- Pound the desiccated coconut and add this to the spice mix.

- Preheat the oven to 200°C (400°F).

- Arrange the chicken pieces in a 28 x 20 x 5-cm (11 x 7 x 2-in) baking dish. Pour the spice paste over the chicken, covering each piece well.

- Cut the turmeric leaf into short pieces. Tear each pandan leaf into long thin strips and tie into a knot.

- Tuck the aromatic leaves around the chicken pieces. Cover the dish tightly with foil and bake in the oven for 1 hour.

- Peel and wash the potatoes. Cut them into smaller pieces and cook in boiling water until tender. Drain well and mash with milk, butter, salt and pepper. Taste and adjust seasoning if needed.

- Once the chicken *rendang* is cooked, let it cool enough to handle. Remove all the aromatic leaves. De-bone the chicken, cutting up any big chunks of chicken meat. Return boned chicken to the *rendang* gravy in the dish.

- Preheat the oven to 200°C (400°F).

- Top the chicken *rendang* with the mashed potatoes. Level the top and sprinkle on the cheese in an even layer. Bake in the oven for about 30 minutes until the cheese forms a golden brown crust.

hae bee hiam cookies

makes about 55

When I was given a box of *hae bee hiam* cookies, I ate the first piece with some apprehension—a savoury, spicy cookie? The initial taste was a little strange, used as I was to the sweet kind of cookies. But I liked it. Somehow the blend of contrasting flavours worked.

To bake the cookies, I decided that they have to be something I could bake on a whim, without having to cook up a batch of *hae bee hiam* first. I considered the ingredients for *hae bee hiam*—shallots, garlic, chillies, dried prawn (shrimp) paste (*belacan*) and, of course, dried prawns (shrimps). The dried prawn paste can be omitted. The dried prawns when fried to a crisp, will replicate the taste of dried prawn paste, which is made of dried prawns after all.

To simplify the process, I fry the dried prawns, sliced garlic and shallots separately until they are crisped through. This will give the cookies an extra oomph, the X factor if you will. The fried ingredients are then pounded finely. A mortar and pestle make easy work of this. Such a small amount of ingredients does not warrant trotting out the blender. The final component is chilli powder. And there you have it—*hae bee hiam*, the cheat's version.

These cookies are an East-West fusion, as well as a successful marriage of old and new. It's a great way to preserve a heritage flavour in the form of a cookie.

Good quality dried prawns (shrimps)	2 Tbsp, about 15 g (1/2 oz)	Unsalted butter	80 g (2 3/4 oz), softened
Shallots	4, peeled	Castor sugar	75 g (2 1/2 oz)
Garlic	1 clove, peeled	Beaten egg	2 Tbsp
Cooking oil	4 Tbsp	Chilli powder	2 tsp
		Self-raising flour	125 g (4 1/2 oz)

- Cut the dried prawns into smaller pieces so they will crisp more evenly. Slice the shallots. The garlic must be sliced rather thinly or it won't crisp properly. These 3 ingredients have to be fried separately as they crisp at different times.

- Heat the oil in a small pan. Fry the shallots until lightly golden. Turn off the flame. Continue to stir the shallots until they turn a light golden brown. Remove and drain on kitchen towels.

- Next fry the garlic slices over a small flame until golden brown. Be watchful as garlic burns easily. Remove and drain on kitchen towels.

- Put the dried prawns in a sieve and rinse quickly under running water. Shake off the excess water, then add to the remaining oil. The dried prawns are washed just before frying so they do not have time to absorb any water. This way they can crisp faster. Fry them over a small to medium flame for about 5 minutes. The flame is just right when there is lots of foaming. If pieces of dried prawns start popping out of the pan, lower the heat. Remove the dried prawns and drain on kitchen towels.

- Let everything cool, then pound the ingredients until fine. Put the pounded ingredients into a mixing bowl.

- Preheat the oven to 180°C (350°F). Line 2 aluminium trays with non-stick baking paper. The bottom of the cookies will brown faster than the top if you use dark coloured trays as these trays absorb more heat.

- Add the butter, sugar, egg and chilli powder to the mixing bowl and mix well. Sift the flour directly into the butter mixture and gently fold it in.

- Drop small dollops (about 1 level tsp) of cookie batter onto the prepared tray, leaving space for the cookies to spread as they bake.

- Bake the first tray of cookies for 12–15 minutes while you prepare the second tray. When the cookies are baked, take them out of the oven and let them cool in the tray for 1 minute before transferring to a rack to cool completely.

- Store in airtight containers. These cookies will keep for 2 weeks.

laksa cookies *makes about 55*

A few years ago, I came across a recipe for laksa cookies in the papers. You had to grind the laksa spices, fry them into a paste, which must be cooled before making the cookies. Needless to say, I never attempted that laborious recipe. Now after trying the *hae bee hiam* cookies, it was a natural progression to use that as a template for laksa cookies. *Hae bee hiam* and laksa share a number of similar ingredients—shallots, garlic, chilli and dried prawns (shrimps). Laksa would require the addition of coconut, turmeric powder and definitely *daun kesom* or what we commonly call "laksa leaf" for that distinctive laksa flavour.

My first attempt produced a cookie that was quite fragrant (how could it not be with all these ingredients?) but not quite tasting of laksa. The second time round—bingo! The cookies really tasted like laksa. A bit disorienting at first but you break out in a smile as you reach for one more, just to be sure of what you are tasting—crispy laksa!

Laksa leaves (*daun kesom*)	80	Unsalted butter	80 g (2³/₄ oz), softened
Good quality dried prawns (shrimps)	2 Tbsp, about 15 g (¹/₂ oz)	Castor sugar	75 g (2¹/₂ oz)
Cooking oil	4 Tbsp	Chilli powder	1 tsp
Shallots	4, peeled, sliced	Turmeric powder	1 tsp
Garlic	1 clove, peeled and thinly sliced	Coconut powder	30 g (1 oz)
		Beaten egg	2 Tbsp
		Self-raising flour	125 g (4¹/₂ oz)

- Wash the laksa leaves. Shake off as much water as possible. Spread them on kitchen towels to dry.

- Cut dried prawns into small uniform pieces so they can crisp evenly.

- Heat the oil over a medium flame and fry the shallots until they start to turn golden. Turn off heat and stir shallots until golden brown. Transfer onto kitchen towels. Fry the garlic over a low flame until lightly browned. Drain on kitchen towels.

- Put the dried prawns in a sieve and wash quickly under running water. Shake off as much water as possible. Add dried prawns to the oil and fry until they become completely crispy, a matter of about 5 minutes. Lower the flame if pieces of prawns start popping out of the pan. The shrimps should fry in oil that is foaming. Remove the fried prawns to drain on kitchen towels.

- Ensure the laksa leaves are dry, then cut them into thin strips.

- Once the shallots, garlic and parwns are cooled, pound them immediately when they are at their crispiest. It is easier to pound them separately. Transfer to a mixing bowl.

- Line 2 baking trays with non-stick baking paper. Turn on the oven to 180°C (350°F).

- Add laksa leaves, butter, sugar, and chilli, turmeric and coconut powders and egg to the pounded ingredients in the mixing bowl. Whisk well to combine.

- Sift the flour directly into the mixing bowl. Gently fold in the flour.

- Shape 1 level tsp of cookie dough into a ball. Use a very light touch to ensure a light crispy cookie. Place the ball on the tray. Continue making these little balls of dough spacing them about 3-cm (1¹/₂-in) apart on the tray. Using the tines of a fork, gently press down on each ball to a thickness of about 0.5-cm (¹/₄-in).

- Bake in the oven for 12–15 minutes. Prepare the second tray of cookies.

- Once the cookies are baked, let them cool in the tray for 1 minute before transferring to a rack to cool completely.

- Store in airtight containers. These cookies will keep for 2 weeks.

jasmine tea cookies *makes about 30*

Jasmine tea-scented cookies are a delightful addition to the Chinese New Year platter of goodies. After the usual and expected spread of staples like pineapple tarts, love letters, almond cookies and *kueh bangkit*, delicious as they all are, it is with a pleasant surprise when you bite into a piece of this jasmine cookie.

Brown sugar	85 g (3 oz)
Unsalted butter	80 g ($2^3/_4$ oz), softened
Salt	$^1/_8$ tsp
Beaten egg	2 Tbsp
Jasmine tea bags	3, about 6 g ($^1/_5$ oz) tea dust
Self-raising flour	125 g ($4^1/_2$ oz)

- Whisk sugar, butter, salt, egg and tea dust together in a mixing bowl.

- Sift flour into the bowl. Gently stir in the flour using a whisk. Do not beat. Remove the whisk. Give cookie dough a final mix with a spatula, stirring any flour on the sides or bottom of the bowl into the mixture.

- Put a piece of cling film on the worktop. Transfer the cookie dough to the cling film. Shape dough into a log about 20-cm (8-in) long. Wrap tightly with cling film and refrigerate for about 2 hours or until the dough hardens.

- Preheat the oven to 180°C (350°F). Line a baking tray with non-stick baking paper.

- Take the cookie dough out from the fridge. Open up the cling film. Slice the dough into 0.5-cm ($^1/_4$-in) thick rounds. Transfer each piece of dough to the tray as you slice, leaving a 2-cm (1-in) gap between the slices.

- Bake for 12 minutes. Remove the tray from the oven and place on a rack. The cookies are very soft at this stage. You will risk breaking them if you try to remove them. Let cookies cool in the tray for a minute before transferring them (with the help of a spatula or palette knife) to the rack to cool completely.

- Store in airtight containers. These cookies will keep for 2 weeks.

chinese peanut cookies *makes about 40*

These melt-in-the-mouth cookies are so easy to do using crunchy peanut butter—a matter of mixing all the ingredients together, rolling the dough into little balls and baking them.

To glaze or not to glaze them is entirely up to you. I tend not to when I bake these cookies for myself, being more concerned with their taste than their appearance. There is the leftover egg after glazing that I have to find some use for—another reason not to glaze. If you intend to, you'll only need about 1 Tbsp of beaten egg. As the cookies are fairly tiny, it is easier to use your finger, dip it into the egg and lightly dab on each cookie.

Crunchy peanut butter	85 g (3 oz)
Cooking oil	2 Tbsp
Castor sugar	75 g (2^1/$_2$ oz)
Self-raising flour	95 g (3^1/$_4$ oz)
Beaten egg (optional)	1 Tbsp

• Line a baking tray with non-stick baking paper.

• Put peanut butter, oil and sugar in a mixing bowl. Whisk them together. Sift the flour directly into the mixture. Using a spatula, mix in the flour until all ingredients are incorporated into a dough.

• Preheat the oven to 180°C (350°F).

• Measure ^{3}/$_4$ tsp of dough by using a ^{1}/$_2$-tsp and a ^{1}/$_4$-tsp measuring spoon. Roll the dough into a ball. This will give you an idea of how big each ball of dough should be. Thereafter you can estimate using the first ball of dough as a guide. If the dough crumbles as you are shaping it, gently knead it a few times first before forming a ball. Place the little balls of dough on the tray about 1-cm (^{1}/$_2$-in) apart. They will expand a little during baking.

• When the entire tray of cookies is ready, glaze with beaten egg if you like.

• Bake for 15 minutes. Take the tray out of the oven. Let the cookies cool completely on the tray. To store, pack them into an airtight container. These cookies will keep for 2 weeks.

coconut and kaffir lime cookies *makes about 32*

The zest and leaves of the kaffir lime give this cookie an interesting citrus taste that is distinctly different from that of the commonly used lime zest in western pastries. The strong aromatic flavour of the leaves mellows upon baking. That is why a fair number of the leaves are needed in this recipe.

To make a spicy version of this cookie, add one big red chilli, finely chopped. For a cookie with a blast, include a finely minced bird's eye chilli on top of the red chilli.

Kaffir lime	1
Kaffir lime leaves	10
Unsalted butter	60 g (2 oz)
Castor sugar	4 Tbsp
Beaten egg	2 Tbsp
Desiccated coconut	20 g ($^2/_3$ oz)
Red chilli (optional)	1, seeded and finely diced
Red bird's eye chilli (optional)	1, seeded and finely diced
Self-raising flour	95 g ($3^1/_4$ oz)

- Line a baking tray with non-stick baking paper.

- Finely grate the rind of the kaffir lime. Cut each kaffir lime leaf in half along the central vein. Remove the central vein of each leaf. Stack the leaves and cut into thin strips.

- Cream the butter, sugar, lime rind and egg together. Mix in the kaffir lime leaves, coconut and chillies (if using). Lastly, sift and fold in the flour.

- Preheat the oven to 180°C (350°F).

- Drop 1 level tsp of cookie dough on the tray. Space the cookies about 2-cm (1-in) apart to accommodate their expansion during baking. There is no need to shape these cookies.

- Bake for 15 minutes until the cookies are lightly golden brown. Remove the tray of cookies from the oven and place on a tray to cool for a minute before transferring the cookies to the rack to cool completely.

- Store in airtight containers. These cookies will keep for 2 weeks.

baking bread

In the whole spectrum of culinary endeavours, there is nothing more satisfying and fulfilling than baking your own bread. It is hard to beat the euphoria of bringing out a beautifully home-baked loaf or a tray of dinner rolls from the oven. I am not referring to bread-baking using a bread machine but kneading and forming the dough by hand.

There is something about the hands-on experience of kneading and shaping the dough that forges this intimacy between bread and baker. The pushing and pulling of the dough, the folding and shaping, the feel of the dough yielding to your touch, working with you—all of which are unique to bread-baking. Why let the bread machine have all the fun?

Although bread-baking takes time, and hence, patience on your part, it is not at all the laborious process you might imagine it to be. Asian bread goes through only one fermentation process, so from start to finish, it requires less time to make than European breads.

Asian bread has a very different crumb texture from its western cousins. It is light and cottony soft. The secret to achieving this feather light texture is the inclusion of bread improver, which also gives the bread a soft thin crust. In baking supply stores, there are two types of bread improver—one for crusty bread and the other for sweet enriched bread. Personally, I prefer my rustic crusty bread to be heavy, with irregular holes in the crumbs. Hence I leave out the bread improver. But for enriched Asian bread, the bread improver is not an option.

Once the Asian bread dough is formed and kneaded, it is left to rest for 15–20 minutes before it is scaled, that is, the dough is cut and weighed. Thereafter, each small piece of dough will be shaped, filled and then set aside to proof until doubled. This short fermentation process explains why Asian breads do not have that well-developed "yeasty" flavour of their western counterparts.

There are some steps I have tweaked to make bread-baking a simpler procedure. When I first started, I kneaded the dough on my tabletop, which made cleaning up a chore. Now I knead the dough in the mixing bowl itself. No mess on the table to clean up! In case you are questioning this heretical departure from the norm, may I remind you that in a bread machine, the dough is kneaded inside the bread pan? To make life even easier, I don't even use the usual mixing bowl. I use a non-stick wok or a huge plastic container—things readily available in the kitchen. The moist dough does not stick to the Teflon coating or the plastic at all! Every bit of flour that you add gets completely absorbed into the dough.

Asian bread dough has higher water and fat content, making the dough rather soft and very sticky. It is extremely difficult to handle with your bare hands. Donning disposable plastic gloves help tremendously as the dough does not stick to the gloves. I knead the dough with my gloved hand leaving the other hand to steady the mixing bowl.

I should mention something about yeast—your essential helper in this whole venture, the one ingredient that quietly but diligently does its work of leavening the dough and giving it that "bread" flavour. The fact that yeast is a living organism can instil an irrational dread in some people. The best antidote to fear is knowledge. So let's find out more about yeast and how it leavens the dough.

Instant dry yeast is used in all the bread recipes that follow. It comes in a small box, which contains five sachets. I recommend dry yeast for the home baker as it works very simply. It has a long expiry date, keeps very well in the fridge and is easy to use.

In the dry form, the yeast looks like tiny granules of sand and is inactive in this state. You activate the yeast with water. Some bread recipes call for the addition of some sugar as "food" for the yeast. The instant dry yeast can be mixed directly into the flour and other dry ingredients before the liquids are added. Once activated, the yeast will come to life. It respires like all other living organisms, and in doing so, releases carbon dioxide that induces the dough to rise. When the bread is baked in a hot oven, the heat will cause an expansion of the carbon dioxide, giving the loaf a further rise and the crumb a lighter texture.

The water added to the yeast should not be too hot, or the heat would kill the yeast. Many recipes call for warm water or specify its temperature. Warm is relative and how many people own a kitchen thermometer? Once again, to simplify things, just use room temperature water or even cold water from the fridge. The yeast will be activated with either. It will take a little longer with cold water, but the dough will still rise. Remember a longer proofing time is desirable if you aim to develop more flavour in the bread.

Be sure to check the expiry date on the box of yeast. Yeast past its shelf life is ineffective and does absolutely nothing for the dough. You want healthy yeast that when activated, is at the prime of its life. In case you want to know—the yeast doesn't bite.

There is much pleasure to be had in shaping the dough, whether you are making a loaf or small buns. You will find that Asian bread dough is smooth, soft and extremely malleable.

Well, that's the long and short of baking bread. Are you ready to bake some now? Let's get to it.

135

nihon curry buns *makes 10 buns*

My friend, Rina, is an ex-teacher turned baker. This spunky lady single-handedly operates a mini bakery in a school canteen selling buns that she makes every morning. Students wait in L-shaped, and sometimes W-shaped queues in front of her stall each day.

A favourite among Rina's young customers, this nihon curry bun is Rina's idea of putting Japanese curry in a neat and convenient package for consumption.

These buns must not be left to cool in the baking tray or the bottoms will turn soggy. Once out of the oven, transfer the buns to cool on a rack. They must be cooled completely before storing.

Filling

Skinless chicken breast	250 g (9 oz)
Carrot	$1/2$, small, about 50 g ($1^2/3$ oz), peeled
Potato	1, medium, about 150 g (5 oz)
Onion	1 small, peeled and finely diced
Cooking oil	1 Tbsp
Curry powder	$1^1/2$ Tbsp
Ground white pepper	$1/4$ tsp
Sugar	2 tsp
Salt	$3/4$ tsp
Water	1 Tbsp

Dough

Bread flour	250 g (9 oz)
Instant dry yeast	1 tsp
Bread improver	1 tsp
Salt	$1/2$ tsp
Sugar	$3^1/2$ Tbsp
Milk	150 ml (5 fl oz)
Beaten egg	2 Tbsp
Unsalted butter	50 g ($1^2/3$ oz), softened
Extra flour	for dusting

Topping

Beaten egg	1 Tbsp
Breadcrumbs	1 Tbsp

- Wrap the chicken and carrot tightly in foil and put on a baking tray. Cook in the oven, set to 180°C (350°F) for 30 minutes. There is no need to preheat the oven. Remove the tray from the oven but leave covered with foil for the ingredients to reabsorb the juices.

- Cook the potato in a small pot for about 30 minutes. Peel and cut into 1-cm ($1/2$-in) cubes.

- Cut the carrot and chicken into 1-cm ($1/2$-in) cubes.

- Over a gentle flame, soften the onion in the oil. When the onion starts to brown, add the curry powder and pepper and fry for a few seconds until fragrant.

- Toss in the potato, chicken, carrot, sugar, salt and water. Cook until mixture is dry. Taste and add more salt and sugar if needed. Transfer to a bowl to cool.

- To form the dough, mix the first 5 dry ingredients in a mixing bowl. Add the milk and egg. Using a spatula, combine the ingredients to form a dough. Put on a disposable glove and knead the dough for a few seconds before kneading in the softened butter, 10 g ($1/3$ oz) at a time. Continue kneading for another 10 minutes. Do not add more flour to the dough as this would upset the moisture content of the dough. Leave the dough to rest for 15 minutes covered with cling film.

- Line two 20 x 30-cm (7 x 11-in) trays with non-stick baking paper.

- Divide the filling into 10 portions, each weighing 50 g ($1^2/3$ oz). Place each scaled portion on some cling film.

- Dust your hands lightly with flour. Divide the dough into 10 portions. Form a piece of dough into a ball, then flatten it so it fits snugly in your cupped hand. Using a spoon, transfer the filling, bit by bit into the dough. With the spoon,

push the filling into the dough gently but firmly to pack the filling as tightly as possible.

- Seal the edges of the dough tightly. Shape the bun into a ball and place on a prepared tray, sealed side up. Space out the buns on the tray.

- Leave the buns to rise until doubled in volume, about 45 minutes–1 hour.

- Preheat the oven to 200°C (400°F).

- Brush each risen bun with the beaten egg, then sprinkle with breadcrumbs.

- Bake each tray of buns for 8–10 minutes. Transfer buns to a rack to cool.

kimchi-pork buns *makes 10 buns*

Rina's nihon curry buns (page 136) were the inspiration for this recipe. As an extension of the Asian theme, it was a natural inclination to consider a Korean bun, with Korea being one of Japan's closest neighbours. And what could be more Korean than kimchi? You can use store-bought or homemade kimchi. If using the latter, make sure it is kimchi that has been allowed to ripen for at least a week in the fridge. This will give a stronger kimchi flavour.

Dough

Bread flour	250 g (9 oz)
Instant dry yeast	1 tsp
Bread improver	1 tsp
Salt	1/2 tsp
Sugar	3 1/2 Tbsp
Milk	150 ml (5 fl oz)
Beaten egg	2 Tbsp
Unsalted butter	50 g (1 2/3 oz), softened
Extra flour	for dusting

Filling

Minced pork	150 g (5 oz)
Salt	1/8 tsp
Sesame oil	1 tsp
Cooking oil	1 tsp
Garlic	1 clove, peeled and minced
Korean chilli powder	2 tsp or 1 red chilli, seeded and finely chopped
Kimchi	250 g (9 oz), roughly chopped

Topping

Breadcrumbs	2 tsp
White sesame seeds	1/2 tsp
Black sesame seeds	1/2 tsp
Beaten egg	1 Tbsp

- Prepare the filling. Combine minced pork with salt and sesame oil. Heat oil and lightly brown garlic. Add chilli powder or chopped chilli and sauté for a few seconds before adding the kimchi. Fry the kimchi until most of the kimchi liquid has evaporated.

- Add the minced pork, stirring and breaking up the clumps of meat as you go. Cook for 1–2 minutes to obtain a moist mixture without a puddle of sauce at the bottom. Transfer filling to a bowl and leave to cool.

- To form the dough, mix the first 5 ingredients in a mixing bowl. Add milk and egg. Using a spatula, combine the ingredients to form a soft dough. Put on a disposable glove and knead the dough for a few seconds before kneading in the softened butter. Once all the butter has been incorporated, continue kneading for another 10 minutes. Do not add more flour to the dough as that would upset the moisture content of the dough. Leave the dough to rest for 15 minutes covered with cling film.

- Line two 20 x 30-cm (7 x 11-in) trays with non-stick baking paper.

- Divide the filling into 10 equal portions, each weighing 50 g (1 2/3 oz). Place each scaled portion on some cling film.

- Dust your hands lightly with flour. Divide dough into 10 portions. Roll a piece of dough into a ball, then flatten so it fits snugly in your cupped hand. Using a spoon, transfer the filling, bit by bit into the dough. With the spoon, push the filling into the dough gently but firmly to pack the filling as tightly as possible.

- Seal the edges of the dough tightly and shape into a ball. Place the finished bun on a prepared tray, sealed side up. Space the buns out on the tray.

- Leave the buns to rise until doubled in volume, about 45 minutes–1 hour.

- In the meantime, mix the breadcrumbs and black and white sesame seeds together.

- Preheat the oven to 200°C (400°F).

- Brush each risen bun with the beaten egg. Sprinkle topping onto each bun.

- Bake each tray of buns for 8–10 minutes. Transfer buns on a rack to cool.

kaya-butter buns *makes 10 buns*

This bun is a marriage of the popular coffee bun (also known as "Roti Boy") and our local breakfast favourite, kaya-butter toast. The sweet kaya (egg and coconut jam) and salted butter are enveloped in soft sweet bread, topped with a crispy coconut-pandan crust. Like the savoury buns in the previous recipes, this sweet one is delicious eaten warm.

Dough

Bread flour	250 g (9 oz)
Instant dry yeast	1 tsp
Bread improver	1 tsp
Salt	1/2 tsp
Sugar	3 Tbsp
Pandan juice (page 13)	3 Tbsp
Milk	105 ml (3 1/2 fl oz)
Beaten egg	2 Tbsp
Unsalted butter	30 g (1 oz), softened
Extra flour	for dusting

Filling

Butter	100 g (3 1/2 oz), cold
Kaya	7 Tbsp

Topping

Unsalted butter	35 g (1 oz), softened
Sugar	55 g (2 oz)
Beaten egg	1 1/2 Tbsp
Coconut powder	1 1/2 Tbsp
Self-raising flour	60 g (2 oz)

- Mix the first 5 ingredients in a mixing bowl.

- Add pandan juice, milk and beaten egg. Use a spatula to mix everything together to form a dough.

- Put on a disposable glove and knead the dough for a few seconds. Now knead in the softened butter 10 g (1/3 oz) at a time. Continue to knead for another 10 minutes. Do not add more flour to the dough as it would upset the moisture content of the dough. Cover the dough and let it rest for 15 minutes.

- Prepare the filling. Cut the butter into 10 g (1/3 oz) pieces. Return the butter to the fridge until needed.

- Divide the *kaya* into 2 tsp portions.

- Line two 30 x 20-cm (12 x 8-in) trays with non-stick baking paper.

- Divide the dough into 10 pieces each weighing 50 g (1 2/3 oz) . Place each scaled portion on some cling film.

- Take the butter out from the fridge.

- Dust your hands lightly with flour. Roll 1 portion of dough into a ball, then flatten it so it fits snugly into your cupped hand. Place a portion of *kaya* and a piece of cold butter into the dough. Gather the edges of the dough upward and seal tightly. This is important as the butter will melt and ooze out while baking if the dough is not properly sealed. Place the bun sealed side up on the prepared tray. Space the buns out on a prepared tray. Leave to rise until doubled in volume, about 45 minutes–1 hour.

- In the meantime, prepare the topping. Cream the butter, sugar, beaten egg and coconut powder together with a spatula.

- Sift the flour directly into the creamed mixture. Gently mix in the flour.

- Transfer the topping into a disposable piping bag.

- When the buns have doubled in volume, turn on the oven to 200°C (400°F).

- Pipe the topping onto each bun in a lattice pattern.

- Bake each tray of buns for 12–15 minutes. Transfer buns to a rack to cool.

garlic-butter and cheese naan *makes 8 naans*

Naan is such a fun bread to bake and eat. The flat piece of dough blisters and puffs up in the oven before your very eyes—how absolutely compelling is that?

Naan is baked without the bread improver, as it isn't the soft cottony type of Asian bread. It is typically baked in a tandoor, which can generate heat of up to almost 500°C (932°F). This intense heat can brown the exterior and cook the dough in a very short time, lessening any moisture loss. When cooking naan in a domestic oven, turn it up to the highest temperature setting. Naan cooks very quickly—about 5–7 minutes. When baked, naan is off-white with a few spots of brown.

Curiously, we don't bite into a piece of naan the way we would a slice of bread. Once the naan comes out of the oven, we brave the heat and instinctively tear it for that first taste. In the case of cheese naan, the fun is doubled. As you tear, the cheese oozes out, fluid and stringy—just like soft, liquid chewing gum.

Bread flour	500 g (1 lb 1 1/2 oz)
Instant dry yeast	1 1/2 tsp
Salt	1 1/2 tsp
Milk	125 ml (4 fl oz / 1/2 cup)
Yoghurt	4 Tbsp
Eggs	2, beaten
Vegetable oil	2 Tbsp
Garlic	4 cloves, peeled and finely grated
Butter	30 g (1 oz)
Mozzarella cheese	300 g (10 1/2 oz)
Coriander leaves (cilantro)	1 large bunch, washed, dried and roughly chopped

- Mix 450 g (1 lb) flour, yeast and salt in a mixing bowl.

- Add the milk, yoghurt, eggs and oil. Using a spatula, draw the dry ingredients into the liquids. You will end up with a somewhat messy looking dough.

- Dust your hands with some of the remaining flour and knead the dough for about 10 minutes, adding more flour little by little until you obtain a smooth elastic dough. You may not use up all the remaining flour.

- Shape the dough into a disc and place into a bowl. Cover the bowl with cling film. Leave the dough to rise until triple its original volume.

- Using a low flame, cook the garlic in a small non-stick pot for 1–2 minutes. If the garlic is drying too fast, add some water and allow the garlic to cook slowly. Now add the butter and fry for a few seconds. Remove from the heat. Do not brown the garlic. If it browns now, it may burn later in the oven and turn bitter.

- If you are using whole pieces of mozzarella, cut it up into 8 portions. If using grated cheese, divide the cheese into 8 parts and then press each portion tightly together to form a disc. When the cheese is packed into a compact disc like this, it will stay soft and molten during the baking. Chill the cheese.

- Cover your worktop with a large sheet of aluminium foil. This is for rolling the dough.

- You will also need 2 large pieces of cling film, which you should also place on the worktop. The rolled out naan will be placed here before baking. The naan will not stick to the cling film.

- Get the following ready:

  - A rolling pin.
  - Extra flour for dusting.
  - The garlic-butter mixture, with a pastry brush.
  - Chopped coriander leaves.
  - Chilled mozzarella.
  - A small dish of water for wetting the dough.
  - A heavy duty tray lined with foil for baking the naan. The drip tray that comes with the oven is very suitable for this purpose. It won't buckle in the fervent heat of the oven. If you haven't got one, then any large baking tray will do.
  - A metal spatula for removing the naan from the oven.
  - A large serving plate or basket for the baked naan.
  - A dry clean piece of dish cloth to cover the naan.

- Now flour your hands. Divide the dough into 8 equal portions.

- Take 1 portion and divide it into 2 equal balls. Roll 1 ball into a small circle. Scatter some coriander leaves on the dough and continue to roll to a diameter of 15–16-cm (6–6$\frac{1}{2}$-in). The coriander leaves will adhere quite firmly to the dough this way.

- Roll out the second small ball of dough into a circle of similar dimensions. Put a piece of mozzarella in the centre of this dough. Moisten the edges with water. Cover with the first piece of dough—the side with the coriander leaves facing up. Press around the edges to seal tightly. Place this piece of naan on the cling film. Repeat this process for the other portions.

- Preheat the oven, with the foil-lined baking tray in it, at 240°C (475°F) or 220°C (425°F) for a fan-assisted oven. The tray needs to be hot to prevent the naan from sticking to it.

- Before putting the naan into the oven, press firmly around the edges of the naan again. Brush each piece of naan generously with the garlic butter.

- Put 2–4 pieces of naan in the oven. Close the oven door immediately and bake for about 5 minutes until they puff up and just begin to brown in spots.

- Transfer the baked naan to the serving dish with a metal spatula. Bake another batch. Cover the baked naan with a clean dishcloth to keep them warm or serve the naan immediately.

pandan bread pudding *serves 6–8*

I have never been fond of bread and butter pudding. It is the one item I invariably pass at any buffet. Frankly I find it a bit boring. Who wants to eat bread for dessert after a full meal? Curiously, French toast, using the very same ingredients of eggs, milk, sugar and bread, is one of my favourite ways to eat bread.

Is there any way to transform this bread pudding into something more exciting? Something more befitting of a dessert status and which does not make you think you're simply eating bread? An Asian bread pudding comes to mind using classic Asian ingredients such as pandan juice in place of vanilla, and coconut milk instead of dairy milk.

The result is a bread pudding wholly worthy to be served as a dessert at the end of an Asian meal. It is fragrant and moist with a texture slightly similar to Nyonya *kueh*. This pudding can be served hot but it is much better cold. It is very soft when hot but will firm up gradually as it cools. Chill this in the fridge, then slice and serve.

You can use any leftover plain sandwich bread. Commercially manufactured bread is much softer and will absorb the egg custard mixture readily. Home-baked bread made without any bread improver has a denser crumb texture and hence requires a longer time to soak up the liquid. But it produces a firmer bread pudding. There is no need to trim the crust which provides more textural interest.

Coconut milk	300 ml (10 fl oz / $1^1/_4$ cups)
Pandan juice (page 13)	4 Tbsp
Eggs	4, beaten
Castor sugar	70 g ($2^1/_2$ oz)
Bread	4 slices, cut into cubes

- Put coconut milk, pandan juice, eggs and sugar in a mixing bowl. Stir gently to dissolve the sugar.

- Add the bread cubes to the egg mixture. Stir to mix well and leave the bread to soak up the custard.

- Preheat the oven to 180°C (350°F). Get ready a 5-cup capacity casserole dish.

- When the oven is ready, pour the bread pudding into the baking dish. Press down the bread cubes into the custard.

- Bake the pudding for about 40 minutes. When a skewer or satay stick is inserted into the centre of the pudding, it should come out clean.

- Cool on a rack and then chill in the fridge. Slice and serve.

durian bread pudding *serves 6–8*

Another Asian take on the bread pudding—this time using the king of fruit—the durian.
   The durian is well-loved by many and brings its distinctive inimitable flavour to this pudding.
Even though I don't enjoy eating durians fresh, I like it cooked and especially when it is used
in a dessert combined with other ingredients.

Coconut milk	250 ml (8 fl oz / 1 cup)
Gula melaka syrup (page 13)	125 ml (4 fl oz / $^1/_2$ cup)
Durian puree	250 ml (8 fl oz / 1 cup)
Castor sugar	2 Tbsp
Salt	$^1/_4$ tsp
Eggs	4, beaten
Bread	4 slices, cut into cubes

- Put coconut milk, *gula melaka* syrup, durian puree, sugar and salt in a mixing bowl. Stir until the sugar is dissolved and the puree is properly mixed into the liquid. Add eggs. Continue to stir until everything is well combined.

- Add the bread cubes to the egg mixture. Stir to mix well and leave the bread to soak up the custard.

- Preheat the oven to 180°C (350°F). Get ready a 5-cup capacity casserole dish.

- When the oven is ready, give the bread pudding another stir and then pour into the baking dish. Press down the bread cubes into the custard.

- Bake the pudding for about 40 minutes. When a skewer or satay stick is inserted into the centre of the pudding, it should come out clean.

- Cool on a rack and then chill in the fridge. Slice and serve.

tropical butter cakes

According to food historians, the early Egyptians baked the first cakes that were rather similar to bread sweetened with honey (sugar didn't exist then). Those creative bakers even added spices and fruit like dates to their cakes—the first fruitcake perhaps?

Cakes have come a long way since. They have evolved into the countless varieties we know today, ranging from simple butter cakes to indulgent multi-layered frosted creations. Although a plain butter cake is at one end of the continuum, it is in no way insipid. Eating a slice of this cake is pure pleasure—the flour, sugar, eggs and butter all meld together magically to form this wonderful baked confection of moist golden buttery crumbs. Butter is the key, the essence, the soul of its flavour.

It is an outrage to see bakeries selling "butter" cakes that do not have a trace of butter in them. Only those who have never tasted a cake made with butter can buy into this conspiracy. Those cakes that are prettily decorated with cream and other adornments don't tempt me either. The cream simply camouflages layers of generic-tasting commercial sponge. A store-bought mango cake comes with the aforementioned sponge and cream with slices of mangoes between the layers and on top. The same goes for durian cakes. When I eat a durian cake, I want the durian in the cake, not on or between it. The artificially flavoured banana cake really raises my hackle. Bananas are plentiful and inexpensive. Is there a need to resort to a synthetic flavouring? Seriously, how difficult is it to mash a couple of bananas and stir that into a basic butter cake batter?

It is guilelessly easy to make a fruit cake flavoured by the real fruit. The simplicity of this got me thinking of using other tropical fruit in butter cakes. The flavours and textures of tropical fruit are as diverse as they are difficult to classify. They are not mere variations of the sweet and sour theme, but range from the light, crunchy and sweet *jambu* (rose apple), the incredibly sweet, soft, almost cooked-potato like texture of the *chiku*, to the creamy, bittersweet yet pungent durian, and everything else in between. Let's not forget the amazing, unique, multi-faceted coconut—a fruit in which every part is used, either for culinary or household purposes.

My recipe for durian marble cake came about when there was a surplus of durians that I was absolutely not going to store in the fridge. Fresh durians, like raw garlic, are offensively assertive in taste and smell, but mellow into the most delightful fragrance and flavour when cooked. The good thing about this recipe is you don't need D24 durians to produce a good cake. Those 'watery' textured durians can be put into good use here.

Chempedak, a tropical fruit similar in texture to the durian, but resolutely different in taste, is another great fruit to use in a cake. But let's not stop at fruit—exotic aromatic Asian ingredients like ginger, pandan and torch ginger buds are all promising possibilities to explore.

So let's have cakes—Asian cakes!

durian marble cake

makes one 22-cm (8¹/₂-in) square cake or one 23-cm (9-in) round cake

Turn your leftover durian into this cake and you won't have to worry about them stinking up your fridge. You need a total of 2 cups of durian puree for this cake. But puree the durian flesh 1 cup at a time. The flesh is quite thick and creamy, so you may experience a bit of difficulty if you try to blend the 2 cups at the same time.

As the butter content of this cake is quite high, any unfinished cake should be kept in the fridge or freezer. The baked cake, tightly wrapped in foil, can be kept in the fridge up to 2 weeks, or frozen for up to a month. Butter cakes taste better the following day and should be eaten at room temperature. Take the cake out from the fridge or freezer and let it come to room temperature. This allows the butter in the cake to soften so the cake will taste soft and moist.

Cake batter A

Durian flesh	250 g (9 oz)
Unsalted butter	250 g (9 oz), softened
Castor sugar	280 g (10 oz)
Eggs	5
Self-raising flour	320 g (11¹/₃ oz)

Cake batter B

Durian flesh	250 g (9 oz)
Egg	1
Gula melaka syrup (page 13)	2 Tbsp
Coconut powder	30 g (1 oz)
Sugar	2 Tbsp
Brown food colouring	a few drops
Self-raising flour	60 g (2 oz)

- Remove the flesh from the durian into a measuring cup. Pack the flesh down firmly to get 1 cup. Puree the first cup of durian flesh and set aside. This is for cake batter A.

- Repeat the above step to obtain a second cup of durian puree for cake batter B.

- Line a 22-cm (8¹/₂-in) square cake tin or a 23-cm (9-in) round one with non-stick baking paper, leaving a slight overhang so cake can be lifted out after baking.

- Preheat the oven to 150°C (300°F).

- Start by preparing cake batter B first. Mix the first 6 ingredients together. Sift the flour into the mixture and fold in gently. Set aside.

- To prepare cake batter A, cream the butter and sugar together with a metal whisk. Whisk in the eggs one at time. Make sure that each egg is properly incorporated before adding the next.

- Mix the durian puree into the butter mixture. Sift 250 g (9 oz) flour directly into the mixture. Still using the whisk, stir the flour gently into the butter mixture. You should not whisk the flour as the vigorous mixing will strengthen the gluten strands in the flour and your cake will not be as

soft. When most of the flour has been mixed in, sift the remaining 375 g (12 oz) of flour into the batter. Once again, stir gently with the whisk. Now change to a spatula. Scrape the sides and bottom of the bowl to finish the mixing job.

- Put half of batter A into the tin. Do not level the batter.

- Add half of batter B, putting globs of it into the craters of batter A. Run a chopstick through the batter to create a marbling effect. Do not over mix or it will result in a homogenous brown batter.

- Repeat with another layer of batter A, followed by B, and then marble those layers with the chopstick.

- Level the top and bake the cake in the preheated oven for 1 hour 50 minutes.

- Let the cake cool in the tin on a rack for 30 minutes first. Remove the cake by lifting up the non-stick paper. Place the cake on the rack to cool completely.

- Slice and serve the cake. Extra portions of cake should be wrapped tightly in foil and kept in the fridge or freezer.

pandan-coconut cake *makes one 22-cm (8¹/₂-in) square cake*

Pandan-coconut cake is quite unlike pandan chiffon cake. This is a butter cake so in terms of flavour, I think it is superior to the chiffon version. The butter makes it more fragrant and moist, with a denser and richer texture. For those of you who are fearful of whipping egg whites, a requirement for chiffon cakes, this is an easier recipe to do—half the work, double the flavour.

Unsalted butter	375 g (13 oz)
Castor sugar	340 g (12 oz)
Coconut powder	1 packet, about 50 g (2 oz)
Green food colouring	1–3 drops, as desired
Eggs	6
Self-raising flour	440 g (15¹/₂ oz)
Pandan juice (page 13)	6 Tbsp

- Line a 22-cm (8¹/₂-in) square cake tin with non-stick baking paper leaving a slight overhang so cake can be lifted out after baking. Preheat the oven to 150°C (300°F).

- Using a whisk, cream the butter, sugar, coconut powder and the green food colouring together in a mixing bowl.

- Add the eggs one at a time, whisking each one well into the butter mixture before adding the next.

- Sift half of the flour directly into the butter mixture. Use your whisk to gently mix in the flour. No more beating now or you'll be working the gluten in the flour and that will reduce the softness of the cake.

- Next, stir in the pandan juice using the whisk. Sift in the rest of the flour and mix in gently. When most of the flour has been incorporated, switch to a spatula to complete the folding in of the flour, scrapping the bottom and sides of the bowl well.

- Transfer the cake batter to the prepared tin. Level the surface and bake for 1 hour 30 minutes.

- Remove the cake from the oven. Place the whole thing on a rack to cool for at least 30 minutes before removing the cake by lifting the non-stick baking paper. Place the cake on the rack to cool completely.

ginger flower muffins *makes 12 muffins*

Most people know the torch ginger bud as the ingredient that gives our local salad *rojak* that extra special zing. The *rojak* seller would ever so economically shave a few slivers of this flower into the salad. Those little bits make all the difference—taking the *rojak* from good to superb. The burst of this flower's unique fragrance can induce a sense of euphoria. It is subtle, intriguing, intoxicating and sublime. The torch ginger bud is certainly the queen among Asian herbs.

I always thought the torch ginger bud was a costly ingredient, judging from the miserly bits you get in a serving of *rojak*. Perhaps the *rojak* seller intends to tease us with a hint of the flower's seductive flavour, inducing us to take one mouthful after another, hoping for another burst of that unforgettably temporal savour.

This delicately pretty flower is sold as a bud, its petals folded tightly together. The flower varies in colour from the lightest blushing pink to a warm orange-pink to a slight maroon-pink. It is strange that the smell of the torch ginger bud does not do it justice. You need to bite into the petal for the release of that ethereal flavour.

Besides our Singapore *rojak*, the torch ginger bud is used in Thai, Peranakan, Malay and even Japanese cuisines. But I have yet to come across its addition in a dessert-type dish. I am very sure that its unique floral flavour would not be amiss in something sweet—a cake, possibly?

You are familiar with the gingerbread man. Now I present to you the ginger flower muffin.

Unsalted butter	125 g (4^1/$_2$ oz), softened
Castor sugar	112 g (4 oz)
Coconut powder	4 Tbsp
Gula melaka syrup (page 13)	2 Tbsp
Eggs	2
Torch ginger buds	2 small buds, shredded
Self-raising flour	125 g (4^1/$_2$ oz)
Milk	2 Tbsp

- Preheat the oven to 180°C (350°F). Line a 12-hole muffin cake tin with paper cases.

- Cream the butter and sugar. Now whisk in the coconut powder. Next add the *gula melaka* syrup and mix well.

- Add the eggs one at a time making sure each one is well incorporated before adding the next.

- Change to a spatula and stir in the shredded ginger buds. Sift the flour directly into the butter mixture and fold in gently. Lastly, fold in the milk.

- Divide batter among the 12 muffins cases. Bake for 20 minutes. Remove the muffins immediately from the oven and leave to cool on a rack.

ginger-pandan muffins *makes 12 muffins*

Sweet potato soup, one of my all-time favourite snacks, was the inspiration for this muffin. This simple and easy-to-cook soup is made by simmering bite-size chunks of peeled sweet potato in a broth flavoured with sugar, ginger and pandan leaves. Surely the pleasing flavours of this soup can be duplicated in a muffin?

I tried a version with pureed sweet potato in the muffin mix but found that it didn't add anything to the taste. I thought of including small cubes of cooked sweet potato instead but decided against it. I don't particularly like its mushy texture in the midst of buttery cake crumbs. A second attempt with just ginger and pandan juices turned out flavourful little olive green muffins. The sweet potato soup taste was instantly recognizable without the arduous labour of adding cooked and pureed sweet potato. Ginger lovers like my mom and sisters love this muffin, especially the ginger icing.

Ginger	2 thumb-size knobs, peeled
Unsalted butter	100 g (3^1/$_2$ oz), softened
Castor sugar	75 g (2^1/$_2$ oz)
Eggs	2
Self-raising flour	125 g (4^1/$_2$ oz)
Pandan juice (page 13)	4 Tbsp

Icing

Ginger	1 thumb-size knob, peeled
Icing (confectioner's) sugar	110 g (4 oz), sifted

- Finely grate the ginger to obtain 2 Tbsp ginger pulp and juice.

- Preheat the oven to 180°C (350°F). Line a 12-hole muffin cake tin with paper cases.

- Cream the butter and sugar. Whisk in the eggs, one at a time.

- Next, sift half the flour directly into the mixture. Fold that in.

- Add the pandan juice and grated ginger, including the juice. Mix that in gently. Sift and fold in the remaining flour.

- Divide batter among the 12 muffins cases. Bake for 20 minutes.

- Cool the muffins on a rack.

- In the meantime, make the icing. Finely grate the ginger to obtain 1 Tbsp juice.

- Add the ginger juice to the sifted icing sugar. Mix well with a spoon to get a fairly stiff paste that is able to hold its own shape. If the paste is too stiff or dry, add a tiny bit more ginger juice (about 2–3 drops). If the icing is too runny, add more icing sugar.

- Put the icing into a disposable piping bag, or just use any clean plastic bag. Tie or seal the bag.

- Frost the muffins only when they are completely cooled. Cut a small bit off the tip of the bag and pipe the icing on the muffins in any desired design.

gula melaka cake *makes one 22-cm (8½-in) square cake*

The West have their maple syrup and Muscovado sugar, we have our *gula melaka* or palm sugar. The addition of *gula melaka* gives this cake a deep luscious sweetness, different from that of sugar. This cake tastes nothing like the pandan-coconut cake although coconut milk and pandan juice are also added to it. I use the packet coconut milk found in the chilled food section of the supermarkets. Coconut milk in cartons or cans will do as well.

Unsalted butter	250 g (9 oz), softened
Castor sugar	140 g (5 oz)
Eggs	5
Self-raising flour	320 g (11⅓ oz)

Gula melaka-coconut syrup

Gula melaka	250 g (9 oz), finely chopped
Pandan juice (page 13)	2 Tbsp
Coconut milk	125 ml (4 fl oz / ½ cup)

- To make syrup, heat *gula melaka* and pandan juice in a small pot over a low flame. When the *gula melaka* has completely melted, turn off the fire. Add the coconut milk. Stir through and leave to cool completely. You should have about 300 ml (10 fl oz / 1¼ cups) syrup.

- Line a 22-cm (8½-in) square cake tin with non-stick baking paper leaving an overhang so cake can be lifted out after baking.

- Preheat the oven to 150°C (300°F).

- Cream the butter and sugar with a metal whisk. Add the eggs one at a time, whisking well before adding the next. When all the eggs are incorporated into the butter mixture, add the *gula melaka*-coconut syrup and whisk to mix properly.

- Now sift half the flour directly into the butter mixture. Using the whisk, mix the flour in gently. Sift in the remaining flour and gently mix that in. Knock as much of the cake batter off the whisk as possible. Change to a rubber spatula and continue to fold any last bit of flour into the batter, scrapping the sides and bottom of the mixing bowl.

- Transfer the cake batter into the prepared cake tin. Level the top. Bake in the oven for 1 hour 15 minutes. Take the cake out of the oven. Leave it on a rack to cool for 30 minutes. Holding the edges of the non-stick baking paper, lift the cake out of the tin. Let the cake cool completely on the rack.

asian banana cake *makes one loaf*

Before we get into this Asian banana cake, let me tell you about the old days. My sisters and I loved to go to the *wayang* shows but not for the Teochew opera that was performed on the huge gaudy stage built on stilts. We made a beeline for the itinerant food stalls that invariably accompanied those *wayang* shows.

The usual suspects were always there. We usually ignored the steamed peanuts stall. The drink stall offered pineapple drinks with chunks of pineapple in the clear icy golden liquid. The drink seller also sold small packets of bite-size sugar cane pieces that you chewed to extract the juices and then spat the pulp out. There was the old man who came on his bike on which was a wooden bucket filled with molten golden candy. He would expertly twirl a dollop of that sticky candy at the end of two sticks to attract the kids.

My favourite was the *kiam sng tnee* (literally salty-sour-sweet) stall which sold everything from all kinds of sweet and tangy pickled fruit to sweet, savoury and spicy crisps. Tough choice! I usually settled for strips of pristine white dried coconut flesh generously dusted with sugar and crunchy banana crisps coated with *gula melaka*. There isn't another banana snack quite like this in the world.

In attempting to make an Asian banana cake, I have chosen to omit the ground cinnamon (normally partnered with bananas) and added *gula melaka* instead. My first taste of this cake brought instant recognition—the memories of those banana crisps came flooding back. I couldn't stop smiling fast enough to take another bite. But be sure to get the genuine *gula melaka* as that is what brings the taste of the banana crisps to this cake. The real stuff has a coconut sweetness and fragrance whereas the imitation ones simply taste like brown sugar.

Unsalted butter	125 g (4$\frac{1}{2}$ oz)
Castor sugar	75 g (2$\frac{1}{2}$ oz)
Eggs	2
Gula melaka syrup (page 13)	4 Tbsp
Mashed ripe bananas	180 g (6 oz)
Self-raising flour	190 g (6$\frac{3}{4}$ oz)

- Line a 23 x 13 x 8-cm (9 x 5 x 3-in) loaf tin with non-stick baking paper. Preheat the oven to 150°C (300°F).

- Cream the butter and sugar together with a whisk. Add the eggs one at a time, beating each egg into the mixture well. Whisk the *gula melaka* syrup into the mixture.

- Add the mashed bananas and mix with the whisk.

- Sift the flour directly into the butter mixture. Using the whisk, stir gently to incorporate the flour. When most of the flour has been mixed in, switch to a spatula for a more efficient job of scrapping the sides and bottom of the mixing bowl to mix in any stray bits of flour.

- Pour the cake batter into the loaf tin and bake for 1 hour. Cool on a wire rack for about 30 minutes before turning out the cake. Place the cake on the rack to cool completely.

fluffy chempedak cheesecake

makes one 22-cm (8^1/$_2$-in) square cake

This cheesecake is for those of you who like the soft, light, moist and cottony texture of Japanese cheesecakes. The *chempedak* gives it an interesting flavour, a change from the more common lemony one.

To attempt this cheesecake, you need to whip egg whites. As you whisk the whites, you are actually incorporating air into it, causing the whites to increase exponentially in volume. It is this air that will give the cheesecake its light fluffy texture while the proteins in the whites coagulate upon baking to give the cake structure.

Whipping whites is not as scary as some might have you believe. Just ensure that the bowl and whisk are scrupulously dry and grease-free. Cream of tartar and sugar are added to stabilise the whipped whites.

You can whisk the whites with an electric whisk or a regular handheld metal whisk powered by your biceps. I use the latter and it takes just 5–8 minutes. It is a good way to work out before eating.

Cream cheese	250 g (9 oz), at room temperature
Eggs	8, at room temperature
Chempedak flesh	125 g (4 oz)
Milk	4 Tbsp
Castor sugar	170 g (6 oz)
Corn flour (cornstarch)	60 g (2 oz)
Cream of tartar	^{1}/$_2$ tsp

• Take the cream cheese and eggs out of the fridge several hours before assembling the ingredients. They need to be at room temperature.

• Line a 22-cm (8^1/$_2$-in) square cake tin with non-stick baking paper. Make sure that the paper extends about 5-cm (2-in) above the rim of the tin to accommodate the cake as it rises.

• Process the *chempedak* and milk in a blender to obtain a smooth puree.

• Separate the egg yolks and whites. Place the whites in a large mixing bowl. The whites have the capacity to increase 8 times their initial volume.

• You will need another mixing bowl to contain the cream cheese with 4 Tbsp sugar. Using a whisk, cream these until the sugar melts. Now whisk in all the yolks, followed by the *chempedak* puree, then add the corn flour. You will get a golden yellow batter. (It is all right to be energetic in stirring in the corn flour, something you would not do with wheat flour. The corn flour does not contain any gluten so there is no fear of developing the gluten and

compromising the texture of the cake.) Set the cream cheese mixture aside.

• Preheat the oven to 150°C (300°F).

• Whip the egg whites together with the cream of tartar until foamy. Add the remaining sugar in three batches, whisking well after each addition until the whites reach the stiff peak stage. The whites will at this point be white, glossy, thick and stiff.

• Switch to a spatula. Scoop about a quarter of the egg whites into the cream cheese mixture and gently fold it in. Repeat with another quarter of the egg whites. Finally fold in the rest of the egg whites. At this stage, the batter will be light and airy.

• Pour the cake batter into the lined tin. Level the top and bake for 1 hour 30 minutes.

• Leave the cake to cool completely in the oven, with the door slightly ajar. The cake will shrink as it cools but the gradual cooling will help prevent too much shrinkage.

• Chill the cake in the fridge for a few hours. This will help to firm up the cake slightly. Slice and serve.

mango and ginger flower crumble *serves 8*

I like the idea of something baked and fruity for dessert. But an apple or blueberry crumble is simply not a fitting end to an Asian meal. Neither is something hot and soupy such as green bean soup, which feels more like afternoon tea. Nyonya *kueh* is a bit heavy—even greed can't compel me to eat more than I would like after a substantial meal. A platter of fruit is good and refreshing, but just a wee bit boring. For a pastry junkie like me, a pastry-cum-fruit last course is a more interesting and thoughtful alternative to merely serving fruit.

So back to crumble, but a tropical one—mango crumble. The Asian theme is further augmented by the addition of coconut and torch ginger bud to the crumble. My preferred choice of mango is the Thai honey mango with its sweet smooth tender flesh. It is the least fibrous of all the mangoes. But you can use any other species of mangoes.

The torch ginger bud should not be sliced thread-thin. It should be thick enough, about 0.2-cm ($1/8$-in) in width. Bite into a shred of torch ginger bud, and its subtly seductive flavour is unleashed, drawing you to take another mouthful of the crumble, seeking to repeat that taste sensation.

There is more than enough crumble in this recipe for eight servings. The extra is good for eating by the spoonful or sprinkled over coconut ice cream.

Mangoes	4, about 300 g ($10^{1}/2$ oz) each	

Coconut cream

Coconut milk	250 ml (8 fl oz / 1 cup)
Castor sugar	2 tsp
Corn flour (cornstarch)	2 tsp

Crumble

Torch ginger bud	1 large or 2 small
Self-raising flour	125 g ($4^{1}/2$ oz), cold
Castor sugar	75 g ($2^{1}/2$ oz)
Desiccated coconut	30 g (1 oz)
Unsalted butter	80 g ($2^{3}/4$ oz), cold

- Prepare the coconut cream. Mix the coconut milk, sugar and corn flour in a small pan. Heat, stirring until the sauce comes to a boil. Cool and chill in the fridge. The sauce will have the consistency of thick cream. Set aside.

- Prepare the crumble. Wash and dry the torch ginger bud. Slice the petals into 0.2-cm ($1/8$-in) thick strips.

- Line a 30 x 22-cm (11 x $8^{1}/2$-in) tray with non-stick baking paper. Preheat the oven to 200°C (400°F).

- Sift flour into a mixing bowl. Add sugar, desiccated coconut and torch ginger bud, and mix together with a spatula.

- Cut the butter into small cubes, about 0.5-cm ($1/4$-in). Rub the butter into the flour mixture, using your fingertips. Seek out the pieces of butter and press them into the flour. You should get a crumbly mixture of small and big crumbs.

- Pour the crumbs onto the prepared tray. Using a very light touch, spread the crumbs in an even layer to fill the tray. Do not press the crumbs.

- Bake in the oven for 18–20 minutes. The edges will brown more than the centre, which would be golden brown. The different shades of brown will give your crumble a more interesting appearance.

- Take the tray out of the oven. Place it on a rack. Immediately use a spoon to break up the crumble while it is soft and malleable. Don't pulverise it though. You are aiming for a mixture of uneven crumb sizes. Leave to cool completely. Store the crumble in a resealable bag or airtight container in the fridge.

- To serve, peel the well-chilled mangoes. Cut the flesh into dices and divide among 8 serving dishes. Top each dish with a generous dollop of the coconut cream, followed by 1–2 Tbsp of crumble. Serve immediately.

coconut custard with gula melaka *serves 6*

A crème caramel made with coconut milk, pandan juice and *gula melaka*, instead of cream, vanilla and caramel? My knees turn weak just thinking about it—some of my favourite dessert ingredients in a cold, silky smooth custard that melts in the mouth. This Asian version is richer than its western counterpart so the small serving size in this recipe is just right.

Eggs	3
Coconut milk	180 ml (6 fl oz / $^3/_4$ cup)
Water	125 ml (4 fl oz / $^1/_2$ cup)
Castor sugar	55 g (2 oz)
Pandan juice (page 13)	1 Tbsp
Gula melaka syrup (page 13)	6 tsp

- Put eggs, coconut milk, water and sugar into a mixing bowl. Stir gently until the sugar is dissolved.

- Pour the mixture through a fine sieve into another bowl. Do not skip this step as it helps to break up the clumps of egg white. Use a spoon to gently ease the last lumps of egg white through the sieve.

- Preheat the oven to 180°C (350°F).

- Arrange six $^1/_2$-cup capacity ramekins or Chinese teacups on a tray. Put 1 tsp of *gula melaka* syrup into each ramekin or teacup. Divide the sieved custard among the ramekins or teacups.

- Bake in the oven for about 20 minutes if using ramekins and about 25 minutes if using teacups.

- Remove the custard from the oven to cool completely. Cover each ramekin or teacup with cling film to prevent drying and chill in the fridge for at least 2 hours.

- To serve, run a knife around the sides of each ramekin or teacup. Place a small serving plate over each ramekin or teacup and overturn the custard onto the plate.

sweet ginger custard *serves 4*

Ginger and pandan leaves add lovely notes of subtle spiciness and fragrance to this delicate custard. Use old ginger for a more penetrating piquancy if desired. This dessert is good hot or chilled.

Once again, making this custard in Chinese teacups will require about 5 minutes more cooking time compared to using ramekins. The latter is bigger and shallower, allowing more surface area of the custard to be exposed to heat hence cooking time is reduced.

Ginger	2 thumb-size knobs, peeled and finely grated
Pandan leaves	2
Water	250 ml (8 fl oz / 1 cup)
Castor sugar	70 g (2^1/$_2$ oz)
Eggs	3, at room temperature

- Put grated ginger in a fine sieve and press with a spoon to extract the juice. You should obtain about 2 Tbsp ginger juice.

- Tear the pandan leaves into long thin strips and tie these strips into a knot. Combine ginger juice, pandan leaves, water and sugar in a small pot. Bring to a boil and remove from heat. Let this ginger syrup cool for 5 minutes.

- Break the eggs into a mixing bowl. Mix the eggs by stirring gently with a spoon. Do not beat to avoid incorporating air into the eggs.

- Preheat the oven to 180°C (350°F). Place 4 ramekins or teacups on a baking tray.

- Discard the pandan leaves. Add about 2 Tbsp of the ginger syrup to the eggs while stirring continuously with a spoon. The stirring is crucial to distribute the hot liquid quickly into the eggs and to prevent the eggs from getting scrambled.

- Repeat with another 2 Tbsp syrup, then gradually pour the remaining syrup while stirring constantly.

- Pass the egg mixture through a sieve back into the pot. Use a spoon to press the last clumps of egg whites through.

- Pour the egg mixture into the ramekins or teacups. Cook in the oven for about 15 minutes if using ramekins or about 20 minutes if using teacups. The custard should be slightly wobbly in the centre.

- Serve hot or chilled.

glossary of ingredients

sauces and pastes

1. Black Prawn (Shrimp) Paste (*Hae Ko*)
This is a dark, almost black thick sauce that is sweet and slightly salty. It is most commonly used to make a very tasty sauce for *rojak*, our local salad.

2. Bottled Sambal *Belacan*
This is a ground spice paste made with chillies, shallots, garlic, dried prawn (shrimp) paste (*belacan*) and dried prawns. The paste is seasoned and fried, making it very easy to use for cooking curries, stir-fries and as a dip. When using bottled sambal *belacan*, make sure that the above stated ingredients are included in the preparation.

3. Dried Prawn (Shrimp) Paste (*Belacan*)
This is made of prawns fermented with salt, then sundried and packed into blocks. It has a pungent smell, is slightly moist, and crumbles when pressed. It is used widely in South East Asian cuisine, especially in curries, sambal and spicy dishes. It is not eaten raw, rather it is usually toasted over a stove fire, or wrapped tightly in foil and baked before combining with raw chillies to make a chilli dip. However, it can be added raw to a spice mixture if the mixture is to be cooked before consumption.

4. Fermented Prawn (Shrimp) Paste (*Cincalok*)
This paste is made of baby prawns mixed with lots of salt and fermented in sealed containers. It is sold in small glass bottles. Fermented prawn paste is extremely pungent and intensely salty. In the old days, a bit of this paste mixed with some sliced chillies and shallots, with rice or porridge constituted a meal. The same mixture, with the addition of some kalamansi lime juice is served as a dip for seafood. Fermented prawn paste is also used as an ingredient in dishes like omelette, stir-fried pork and also in kimchi. As it is really salty, a little goes a long way.

5. Prawn (Shrimp) Paste (*Ha Cheong*)
This is a smooth paste made from prawns fermented in salt. It is usually used as a marinade for fried chicken.

6. Essence of Chicken

This is the flavoursome liquid derived from cooking a chicken without the addition of water. It is, in actual fact, a concentrated chicken broth. The commercial version includes the addition of caramel, which gives the essence its clear brown tone.

7. Salted Soy Beans (*Tau Cheo*)

These are soy beans that are fermented in salt. It is not pungent like fermented prawn paste (*cincalok*). Instead it is earthy and salty. Salted beans are usually sold in bottles or jars with the liquid they are fermented in. They can be used with the liquid as a dip for seafood or the beans can be mashed with the liquid to form a paste. A close substitute is miso paste.

8. Tamarind Paste

Tamarind paste is the tangy pulp from the pod of the tamarind tree. It is used in many local dishes that require a sour element to the taste. The tamarind paste is packed together with the seeds into a packet. To use, rub the tamarind paste in water to release the seeds. Strain this and discard the seeds and any fibre. Use the strained tamarind juice as specified in the recipe.

9. Tandoori Spice Paste

This is a mixture of various ground spices like chillies, ginger, cardamom and cumin. The commercially packaged pastes are usually coloured the characteristic red of tandoori chicken. But the fresh tandoori spice paste purchased from the wet market is devoid of artificial colouring.

10. Tom Yum Paste

This is a concentrated paste made with ingredients like lemongrass, galangal, kaffir lime leaves and chillies. It is seasoned and fried in oil, making this very easy to use.

leaves, stems and fruit

11. Bay Leaves
Fresh bay leaves are milder in flavour than the dried ones. Bay leaves add earthy, non-assertive notes to the dish they are cooked in.

12. Coriander Leaves and Roots
Coriander, or cilantro, is another herb that is widely used in Asian cuisines, especially in Thai cuisine. Many Thai dishes also make use of the roots which are cleaned of any soil, and then finely pounded. The leaves, stalks and roots can be eaten raw in a salad. The pretty raw leaves are often used as a garnish for seafood dishes. Their fresh green taste goes fabulously well with such dishes too.

13. Curry Leaves
Tear a curry leaf and its distinctive aroma immediately hits you. Added to any curry, the leaves would give the dish that unmistakable Indian curry flavour. But their culinary usage is much wider. They are an indispensable addition to the creamy butter sauce served with crabs. Here the leaves surprisingly do not make the sauce taste like curry; instead they impart an extra special fragrance to the sauce.

14. Galangal
Like ginger, galangal, or *lengkuas* in Malay, is a rhizome or underground stem. However it does not have the spicy heat of the ginger. It is harder and less juicy. Older galangal can be quite fibrous, hence it is good to thinly slice the galangal to shorten the fibres considerably before pounding it with other spices.

15. Ginseng Roots
Ginseng roots have been used in traditional Chinese medicine for hundreds of years. They are reputed to have amazing health-nourishing properties. In the culinary realm, ginseng roots are used mostly in the preparation of soup tonics. They can be sliced or used whole. Ginseng roots are sometimes combined with other Chinese herbs and braised together with either chicken or pork to make soups. Once cooked, the ginseng becomes tender and is usually consumed with the soup.

16. Kaffir Lime
The kaffir lime is not known to be juicy. Rather, the prized part of the fruit is its rind that has a refreshing citrus flavour. The rind is traditionally grated and used in Thai dishes.

17. Kaffir Lime Leaves
Like the rind of the kaffir lime, the leaves are the other flavoursome part. They are often what give Thai food that citrusy taste. These leaves can be used whole in soups or stews. Lightly crushing the leaves in the palm of your hands helps release their flavour. When used whole, the leaves are not consumed. They can also be finely shredded and added to curries or salad dressings.

18. Torch Ginger Bud
Also known as *bunga kantan* in Malay, these flowers are actually buds of the ginger plant. The beautiful pink petals are tightly folded together, with the inner petals being a deeper pink. The most commonly known use of the ginger flower is in *rojak*, our local salad. Thinly sliced slivers of the petals are added to the *rojak*. The entire bud and part of the stalk are cooked in Penang laksa gravy giving it that heady floral fragrance. The shredded petals are then sprinkled on top of a bowl of this laksa. The taste of this flower is so special, there is no substitute. These flowers are also rarely found in supermarkets. They can only be purchased in some wet markets.

19. Kalamansi Limes

Kalamansi limes are small limes about the size of a huge marble. They are thin-skinned and very juicy although the juice is less sour than that of lemons. Kalamansi limes are squeezed over grilled seafood to add a tangy note as well as to cut the richness of such dishes. They can be mixed with chillies, garlic and soy sauce to be served as a dip. The juices, combined with sugar syrup, water and ice make a very delicious and refreshing tropical drink.

20. Laksa Leaves

Laksa leaves, also known as Vietnamese mint, or *daun kesom* in Malay, have a fresh unique flavour. It lends its distinctive taste to the local dish, laksa, hence its name. The leaves are thinly shredded and used as a topping for laksa. It is also included as one of the herbs in *nasi ulam*, a Malay rice dish. The fibrous stems, though not eaten, can be cooked in the laksa gravy to infuse it with more of that special flavour.

21. Lemongrass

Lemongrass has that pleasing mix of both earthy and lemony notes. The most tender part of the lemongrass lies 5–6-cm (2–3-in) from the root end. This is the part that is often thinly sliced and added to salad dressings or pounded in a spice mix. But do not discard the rest. They will impart flavour to any stew or soup.

22. Limes

Shaped like a lemon, and only slightly smaller, the lime has an refreshingly tart taste that evokes sunshine and tropical gardens. Its rind and juice are flavourful and used in cakes and pastries. The juice can also be made into limeade.

23. Pandan Leaves

Pandan leaves are also known as screwpine leaves. They have a unique flavour that we have come to love in many local desserts. In fact, pandan leaves are to local desserts what vanilla pods are to Western ones. There is no substitute for pandan leaves. The long leaves are too fibrous to be consumed. They are often added (tied into a knot) to sweet soupy desserts. The leaves are also ground and the dark green juice extracted to be used in local cakes and *kueh*, giving both flavour and colour to these desserts.

24. Preserved Mustard Greens

Also known as *mei cai*, preserved mustard greens
are available in two forms: sweet and salty. Both
are dried and then preserved and fermented with
salt; sugar is added to the sweet version. They must
be thoroughly washed to remove all soil and grit.
Leaving them to soak after washing will help to draw
out more salt.

25. Spring Onions

Spring onions are also known as scallions or green
onions. Both the green and white parts can be eaten
either raw, or cooked. They are often diced and
sprinkled onto cooked food or soup as garnish.

26. Turmeric Leaves

Turmeric leaves sold in the market can range from
a palm size to almost a foot long. When cooked, it
renders a fresh, fragrant floral flavour to curries that
immediately makes one think of Malay curries. Indeed
this herb is widely used in Malay cuisine.

dry ingredients

27. Black Fungus
This is a type of cloud ear fungus. When hydrated, it will swell to several times its dried form. Black fungus is used in savoury cooking. They have a slight woody taste with a crunchy texture.

28 Black Glutinous Rice
This rice is used in many local desserts. The rice requires soaking, preferably overnight to aid in speedier cooking. It takes a much longer time than white glutinous rice or regular rice to soften.

29. Bonito Flakes
These are the thin shavings of the dried skipjack tuna. Bonito flakes are used to make soup stock in Japanese cuisine. They are also sprinkled onto dishes for both flavour and aesthetics. Packets of these flakes can be found in the Japanese section of most supermarkets.

30. Cardamom Pods
Cardamom pods are added whole to pilaf and curries. Ground cardamom contribute to the complex flavour of many curry pastes. They are also used to flavour tea.

31. Chinese Red Dates
Red dates are dried Chinese dates that have both medicinal and culinary uses. If the dates are to be consumed, be sure to buy pitted dates or have the seeds removed first. They are usually cooked in soups and even porridge, imparting a mild sweetness to the dish.

32. Chinese Wolfberries
These are the sundried bright red fruit of a plant known as boxthorn. They used to be sold only in Chinese medicine shops. But as their usage extends increasingly in the culinary arena, they can now be found in supermarkets in the dry goods section. The wolfberries can be added directly to soups and rice porridge and cooked together.

33. Cinnamon Sticks
Cinnamon sticks are from the bark of the cinnamon tree. They are used in both western and Asian cuisines, in sweet as well as savoury dishes.

34. Cloves
Cloves are actually the dried flower buds of the clove tree. Cloves may be tiny but they pack lots of flavour. They are used in many cuisines in both sweet and savoury dishes.

35. Coriander Seeds and Powder
The seeds are rarely used whole, but are usually first dry roasted or fried to bring out their flavour, and then ground. Coriander powder is an essential component of many curry spice mixtures.

36. Cumin Seeds and Powder
Cumin seeds are used whole in several Indian dishes like dhal curries and the crispy fried snack, *muruku*. Cumin powder is an indispensable part of many Malay, Indian and Indonesian curries. Cumin is also widely used in Mexican and Middle-eastern cuisines.

37. Dried Scallops
Dried scallops come in a variety of sizes with the smallest ones being the most inexpensive. The small ones can be added directly to soups, stews and porridge to be cooked together.

38. *Gula Melaka*
Gula melaka or palm sugar is made from sap derived from the flower buds of palm trees. It usually comes in round discs. *Gula melaka* tastes like a cross between brown sugar and coconut. Brown sugar can be substituted as a last resort, but it will be missing the fragrant coconut flavour.

39. Herbal Chicken Spices
Herbal chicken spices are made up of a variety of Chinese herbs like wolfberries, ginseng and Chinese angelica. Some brands are milder while others are stronger in taste. Sample different brands to find one that best suits your liking.

40. Sago Pearls
These little white balls are made from tapioca starch. When cooked in water, they increase in size and become translucent and gelatinous. They are usually used in desserts.

41. Turmeric Powder
Turmeric powder is obtained from turmeric or yellow ginger. It is a deeply yellow underground stem. Turmeric does not have the spiciness of ginger. It is used in curries, giving them that lovely sunshine yellow.